English spelling:

Roadblock to reading

Godfrey Dewey, Ed.D.

TEACHERS COLLEGE PRESS
Teachers College, Columbia University
New York

Contents

Contents

Abbreviations
(arranged in alphabetic order)

APA	American Philological Association
Hws	*How we spell! or English heterography* (Dewey)
IAL	International auxiliary language
IPA	International Phonetic Association
i.t.a.	Sir James Pitman's Initial Teaching Alphabet
i.t.m.	initial teaching medium (generic term, including i.t.a.)
NEA	National Education Association
NS	New Spelling (of the British SSS)
RF/Sounds	*Relativ frequency of English speech sounds* (Dewey)
RF/Spellings	*Relative frequency of English spellings* (Dewey)
SRA	Spelling Reform Association
SSA	Simpler Spelling Association
SSB	Simplified Spelling Board
SSS	Simplified Spelling Society
T.O.	traditional orthography
WES	World English Spelling (of the SSA)

Foreword

In this book, *English spelling,* significantly subtitled *Road-block to reading,* the author makes an appropriate addition to his previous uniquely lucid writings on what may justly be described as the basic pedagogical problem of modern and future education, not only in the English-speaking world, but also, in view of the strong appeal of English as the most promising candidate for selection as the world's second language, for all peoples.

While English is already the nearest to a worldwide *spoken* language, our traditional orthography not only handicaps English as a world *written* language, but in our own and other English-speaking nations puts an intolerable and too often traumatic burden on beginning learners. Even among those of our children and adults who do not become nonreaders, the traumas of an irrational alphabet often continue as hidden or unconscious antipathies for, and roadblocks to, effective reading habits, and even more effective roadblocks to writing. Nonreaders not only feel declassé, but also too frequently become victims of frustrations leading to delinquency, crime, and the self-destructive violence associated with political infantilism and susceptibility to demagoguery.

Our multiple debts to Godfrey Dewey, famous son of a famous father, are too numerous to mention in this brief foreword. In this book, as in several previous publications, he writes as Vice-President of the Lake Placid Club Education Foundation and Secretary of the Simpler Spelling Association, formed in 1946 by a merger of the Spelling Reform Association (founded in 1876) and the Simplified Spelling Board (founded in 1906), to which Andrew Carnegie gave more than

$250,000. His manifold interests and activities have included, however, in addition to his lifetime association with the Lake Placid Club in various capacities, such positions as President of the Organizing Committee for the III Olympic Winter Games, Lake Placid, 1932; President of Emerson College, 1949–1951, including a Freedoms Foundation award for his 1950 baccalaureate address; President, 1951–1961, of Forest Press, Inc., publishers of the Dewey Decimal Classification; and Chairman of the Board of Trustees of Northwood School, 1954–1959. His writings have included, among other items, an unpublished Harvard Ed.D. thesis, "A sistem of shorthand for general use," which eventuated in the published Dewey Shorthand textbooks; also numerous published articles, chiefly on shorthand and spelling reform.

While no knowledgeable person can fail to recognize and pay due homage to Godfrey Dewey's long, scholarly, dedicated leadership in the spelling reform movement, tenacious even when it seemed a lost cause, most contemporary workers in the vineyard would probably agree that his most basic and enduring contribution has been his meticulous study and analysis of English speech sounds, published as *Relativ frequency of English speech sounds,* by Harvard University Press, 1923, 1950, and still the accepted authority in that particular field. Its value has recently been substantially enhanced by his companion study of the graphemes of the same material, *Relative frequency of English spellings,* recently published by Teachers College Press. Incidentally, his compilation of the multiple spellings of English phonemes and multiple pronunciations of those graphemes, *How we spell! or English heterography,* first published in 1923, most recently in 1969, and now included as an appendix to this volume, quite fully justifies the adjective used by Noah Webster when he described our traditional spelling conventions as "vicious."

But for this timely, scholarly, and immediately useful book, all of us who are in educational work will feel especially grateful, for in it Dr. Dewey provides — for administrators, authors and publishers of textbooks, and classroom teachers — authentic data and practical suggestions that will help them mitigate the intolerable impact of our irrational traditional orthography, on teachers as well as on pupils, and help our whole educational system to make the adjustments that are prerequisite to assuring all normal children of what former Commissioner James E. Allen, Jr., has so aptly called "the right to read" — a right which, in view of our contemporary civilization and world ecology trends, is considered by our most clear-headed thinkers and Promethean statesmen as equal in importance to any of the rights specifically guaranteed in our Constitution.

It is a privilege to hail this latest contribution from one of our most gifted scholars, whose clarity of ideas and lucidity of expression match the strategic importance of his subject.

> Ben D. Wood
> Director
> Bureau of Collegiate Educational Research

Columbia University
June 1971

Preface

My recently published study, *Relative frequency of English spellings* (hereinafter cited as *RF/Spellings*),[1] was undertaken to provide authoritative objective data on the relative frequency of occurrence, in good English as used today, of the multifarious phoneme-grapheme correspondences of English: that is, the spellings of sounds and the pronunciations of spellings. It thus seeks to do for the graphemes of English substantially what my earlier study, *Relativ frequency of English speech sounds* (hereinafter cited as *RF/Sounds*),[2] did for the phonemes of English, employing, to facilitate comparison, the same 100,000 words of well-diversified connected matter adequately representative of good English as used — written, spoken, or printed — today.[3] The present work is primarily concerned with applying these objective data, in the light of a lifetime of active concern with the problems of English spelling, to the most discussed and fundamentally the most important problem of elementary education — learning to read and write.

Since this is a forward-looking rather than a backward-looking study, I shall touch on the past history of English spelling and of spelling reform only so far as may provide helpful background for the future. For the linguistic scholar, abundant material on both topics is readily available. I am here addressing myself rather to the educator, the textbook author or publisher, and/or the classroom teacher, whose immediate concerns are not with the record of yesterday but with the press-

---

[1] New York: Teachers College Press, 1970.

[2] 2d ed.; Cambridge, Mass.: Harvard University Press, 1950.

[3] For complete list of sources, see *RF/Sounds*, Table 1, pp. 8–9.

ing problems of today and tomorrow. For them I have sought to provide authentic data and practical suggestions for their use in mitigating the present impact of our traditional orthography (hereinafter referred to as T.O.) on the teaching of reading and writing, and eliminating its future impact thru the "final solution," spelling reform.

Acknowledgments are due to Harvard University Press for permission to draw freely on my earlier study, to the Initial Teaching Alphabet Foundation (and to The Bobbs-Merrill Co., Inc., who reprinted in *Education* one section of the same material), to the *International Language Reporter* (formerly, *International Language Review*), and to the International Reading Association for permission to reprint, with or without revision, material from various papers of mine previously published by them. Earlier drafts of several items have also been published in the *Spelling Progress Bulletin*.

To Dr. Abraham Tauber I am indebted for prepublication references to his forthcoming *English spelling reform: Linguistic engineering for better reading, writing, and speaking.* To my long-time friend and coworker in linguistic fields, Sir James Pitman, I am indebted not only for important quotations from *Alphabets and reading,* but especially for his successful initiative and drive in bringing the concept of a phonemic notation as an initial teaching medium, more particularly the Initial Teaching Alphabet (i.t.a.), out of the realm of theory into active and successful accomplishment. Finally, I must once more acknowledge my great indebtedness to that veteran educational reformer, Dr. Ben D. Wood, who has himself rendered invaluable service in this field, and whose interest and helpfulness have encouraged the completion and publication in permanent form of the results of this considerable labor.

Godfrey Dewey

Lake Placid Club, N.Y.
June 1971

English spelling:
Roadblock to reading

Chapter 1

English spelling: Historical background

English spelling has been a problem ever since written representation of the English language began to take definite shape. As early as the 14th century, Chaucer lamented in *Troilus and Criseyde:*

> And for ther is so grete dyversite
> In English, and in writyng of our tonge,
> So preye I God, that non myswrite the,
> Ne the mysmetere for defaut of tonge.[1]

And, as early as the 16th century, commonly taken as the beginning of the modern English period, the first spelling reformers had appeared. John Hart, writing in 1554 and again in 1570, when he published "A Method of Comfortable Beginning for All Unlearned," was the first to emphasize spelling reform as an aid in learning to read;[2] a statement strikingly suggestive of the philosophy of Sir James Pitman's Initial Teaching Alphabet (i.t.a.) today. Likewise, William Bullokar, who about 1580 published four books in his "amended" spelling, made the point that for "easy conference" the new orthography must not differ too much from the old[3]—a statement no less suggestive of today's emphasis on compatibility of an initial teaching medium (hereinafter referred to as i.t.m.) with traditional orthography (herein-

---

[1] Geoffrey Chaucer, *Works* (Boston: Houghton-Mifflin Co., 1957), p. 479.

[2] Abraham Tauber, *English spelling reform: Linguistic engineering for better reading, writing, and speaking* (in preparation; New York: Philosophical Library), Ch. 2.

[3] *Ibid.*

after abbreviated to T.O.) as an aid to transition to the latter.

The fundamental cause of our present chaotic and indefensible spelling, underlying all the rest, has been the effort to spell a cosmopolitan language—basically Anglo-Saxon or Teutonic but greatly enriched from Romance sources, notably Norman-French—which distinguishes about 40 sounds, by means of a Roman alphabet, quite adequate for Latin, for which it was developed, but containing a maximum of 26 letters. In fact, during much of the formative period this alphabet contained only 22 letters, lacking distinction of *j* from *i*, of *k* from *c*, of *u* from *v*, and the character *w*. Thus, the early scribes were compelled to struggle, valiantly but individualistically, lacking any unifying authority, with the problem of expressing alphabetically—so far as might be, phonetically—some 40 sounds with only 20-odd characters. A most interesting as well as scholarly account of the evolution of the Roman alphabet, both upper case and lower case, and of the forces which led to the abandonment, even before the impact of printing, of the Anglo-Saxon characters which might have saved the day, is that of Sir James Pitman.[4]

To touch very briefly on the more important secondary factors which have contributed to the evolution of the spellings with which we are burdened today, the advent of printing developed gradually but somewhat prematurely, while the evolutionary process was still going on, a demand for uniformity, at the same time that it introduced new problems of its own. Many of Caxton's and other early printers were foreigners, especially Dutch, relatively unfamiliar with English, who tended to solve spelling problems, when they recognized them, according to the canons of their own language. Furthermore, until well into the 16th century the practice persisted of justifying lines (straightening the right-hand margin) by adding extra letters rather than spaces—most often a final *e*.

Publication of the King James Version of the Bible in 1611 exerted a powerful influence toward investing with a certain authority the relatively consistent spellings it employed, and to that extent tended to slow down the natural process of attempting to conform current spelling to those changes in pro-

---

[4] Sir James Pitman and John St. John, *Alphabets and reading* (London: Sir Isaac Pitman & Sons, Ltd., 1969), especially Ch. 5.

nunciation which are an inevitable accompaniment of the life and growth of any language. When to this influence was added the ponderous prestige of Johnson's dictionary,[5] appearing in 1755, it may fairly be said that rigor mortis had set in, and that a dead spelling had ceased to attempt to represent faithfully a living language.

Between these dates, one other significant factor had entered in to pollute the well of English undefiled. The scholars and pedants who, inspired by the Renaissance, delighted to trace all good things back to classical sources had devoted some scholarship, and more pseudoscholarship, to discovering classical etymologies for English words and attempting to signalize them in current English spellings. To them we owe such spellings as *comptroller, debt, delight, foreign, island, sovereign,* etc., which in each case conceal the true derivation.

Such further slight changes as have occurred in the last two centuries, including the divergencies between British and American usage for which Noah Webster was chiefly responsible, have been due chiefly to conscious and deliberate efforts at reform (briefly discussed in Chapter 3), rather than to any clearly discernible social or linguistic trends.

[5] Samuel Johnson, *A dictionary of the English language* (London: J. & P. Knapton, 1755).

Chapter 2

English spelling: Present structure

A wholly simple phonemic spelling of English would have only one grapheme corresponding to each phoneme, and only one phoneme corresponding to each grapheme. Our currently accepted T.O. is deficient in that it has only 26 letters, 3 of which (*c q x*) are for all practical purposes duplicates, to represent about 41 sounds – probably the optimum number for a phonemic notation for general use. Largely in consequence of this deficiency, it is also defective in having a multiplicity of spellings for the sounds, and a multiplicity of pronunciations for the spellings. Several symbols for one sound are a major obstacle to *writing* (more particularly, spelling); several sounds for one symbol are a major obstacle to *reading*. The impact of this confusion is the most obstructive single factor in elementary education – in effect, a roadblock to reading, which is not only itself the most important subject of elementary education but also the medium thru which much of the rest of elementary education is carried on.

The simplest statement of the present structure of T.O. will be an examination of the different spellings of the phonemes of English and the different pronunciations of the corresponding graphemes. The examples summarized in Tables 1 and 2, and itemized in Appendixes A and B, are all taken from a single abridged dictionary. They have been published separately under the title, *How we spell! or English heterography* (hereinafter cited as *Hws*).[1]

Elsewhere I have reported at length on the relative fre-

---

[1] Godfrey Dewey, *How we spell! or English heterography* (Lake Placid Club, N.Y.: Lake Placid Club Education Foundation, 1968, 1969).

6

quency of occurrence of phonemes[2] and of graphemes[3] in connected matter. The data here presented do not concern themselves with this aspect, except that the columns headed *RF/Sp* in Tables 1 and 2 reveal that about 2/3 of all spellings and/or pronunciations reported on a dictionary basis are common enough to have occurred at least once in the 100,000 running words on which my studies of relative frequency were based.

Elsewhere,[4] also, I have discussed two similar studies, those by Ellis in 1842 and Pitman (and St. John) in 1969, which, by more liberal criteria which include not only proper names but also definitions of spellings which often count the same irregularity twice and occasionally three times, arrive at substantially larger totals; and have expressed my judgment that my more restrictive criteria, reproduced immediately preceding Appendixes A and B, give a juster and quite sufficiently appalling measure of the chaos with which we have to deal.

Tables 1 and 2, with comments, follow on pages 8–12.

How phonemic is English spelling?

How phonemic is our present English spelling? For a variety of reasons, no simple direct answer to our question is possible, and statements which fail to define their terms clearly are either meaningless or misleading — usually both.

In the absence of acceptable criteria, answers by others to our question, how phonemic or phonetic or "regular" (a term that, like charity, can be stretched to cover a multitude of sins) is English spelling, range all the way from Hotson, "At present we use 500 symbols for 40 sounds, so that English is 8% phonetic," [5] to Spalding, "If properly studied and taught, our language is, in fact, almost completely phonetic or regular," [6] based on her statement that 94% of the most used 1,000

---

[2] Dewey, *RF/Sounds*.

[3] Dewey, *RF/Spellings*.

[4] *Ibid.*, Ch. 1.

[5] Clarence Hotson, Ph.D., *Ryt Ryting* (Romulus, N.Y.: Privately printed, 1965), p. 6.

[6] Romalda B. Spalding, in *Reading Reform Foundation Conference Proceedings* (New York, 1964), p. 31.

Table 1 Summary of spellings of sounds*

| | Consonants | | | | Vowels | | |
| | Traditional spellings | | Phonemic spelling | | Traditional spellings | | Phonemic spelling |
Sound	Total	RF/Sp		Sound	Total	RF/Sp	
p	5	2	1	a	13	4	1
b	5	2	1	ɑ	16	9	1
t	14	9	1	e	19	10	1
d	7	4	1	ɑ	36	19	1
k	17	11	1	i	33	20	1
g	6	4	1	ɛ	23	20	1
f	8	7	1	ɒ	11	7	1
v	8	4	1	ɔ	17	13	1
ħ	4	2	1	ʊ	13	10	1
ħ	2	1	1	o	23	19	1
s	17	9	1	u	12	11	1
z	13	7	1	ɯ	29	19	1
ʃ	20	15	1	ə	43	23	1
ʒ	10	5	1	ɑ́	22	14	1
ʤ	7	5	1	aɪ	7	3	1
j	12	10	1	ɟ	7	5	1
m	8	5	1	ɪɯ	18	10	1
n	14	9	1		342	216	17
ŋ	3	3	1		219	145	24
l	7	7	1		561	361	41
r	11	10	1	ƀə			1
w	10	5	1				362
y	8	6	1				
h	3	3	1				
	219	145	24				

RF/Sp = Number found in 100,000 running words in *RF/Spellings*.

* See Appendix A.

The foregoing summary reveals:

In our traditional orthography —
219 spellings/24 consonants = 9.1 spellings per sound
342 spellings/17 vowels   = 20.7 spellings per sound
561 spellings/41 sounds   = 13.7 spellings per sound

In a phonemic notation —
41 spellings/41 sounds   = 1   spelling per sound

To point up the significance of these figures, consider a simple 5-letter word like *taken*. By analogies with the examples here given, this might be spelled in any one of $14 \times 36 \times 17 \times 43 \times 14 = 5{,}157{,}936$ different ways. One might be *phtheighchound* (compare *phth*isic w*eigh* s*ch*ool glam*our* ha*nd*some). In a phonemic notation only one spelling would be possible — in the SSA phonemic alphabet, Table 6, *takən* (in World English Spelling, Table 5, *taeken*).

Table 2   Summary of

Initial letter	TOTALS				Single letters			
	Totals Spel/Pron		RF/Sp Spel/Pron		Totals Spel/Pron		RF/Sp Spel/Pron	
a	24	74	18	40	1	9	1	8
b	5	5	3	3	1	1	1	1
c	16	23	9	13	1	5	1	3
d	9	11	6	8	1	3	1	3
e	32	77	24	54	1	7	1	6
f	3	4	3	4	1	2	1	2
g	9	16	6	10	1	3	1	3
h	9	15	6	7	1	2	1	2
i	14	38	14	24	1	7	1	5
j	2	4	1	1	1	3	1	1
k	3	3	2	2	1	1	1	1
l	11	15	8	9	1	3	1	2
m	6	8	4	4	1	1	1	1
n	7	10	4	6	1	2	1	2
o	37	88	23	60	1	9	1	8
p	10	13	7	7	1	1	1	1
q	1	1	1	1	1	1	1	1
r	10	12	8	9	1	1	1	1
s	17	30	10	18	1	4	1	4
t	10	17	8	12	1	3	1	3
u	21	52	14	43	1	9	1	8
v	3	3	2	2	1	1	1	1
w	4	7	4	5	1	2	1	1
x	3	11	3	10	1	3	1	2
y	6	11	3	6	1	5	1	4
z	8	13	2	4	1	4	1	3
	280	561	193	362	26	92	26	77

RF/Sp = Includes spellings and/or pronunciations found in 100,000 running words in *RF/Spellings*.

° See Appendix B.

† Includes wordsign *the*.

pronunciations of spellings *

Simple digraphs				All other †				Initial letter
Totals		RF/Sp		Totals		RF/Sp		
Spel/Pron		Spel/Pron		Spel/Pron		Spel/Pron		
9	34	9	16	14	31	8	16	a
4	4	2	2					b
9	12	7	9	6	6	1	1	c
7	7	5	5	1	1			d
11	39	10	27	20	31	13	21	e
2	2	2	2					f
7	11	5	7	1	2			g
5	9	3	3	3	4	2	2	h
5	15	5	8	8	16	8	11	i
1	1							j
2	2	1	1					k
8	9	7	7	2	3			l
4	5	3	3	1	2			m
5	6	3	4	1	2			n
10	32	10	26	26	47	12	26	o
6	8	5	5	3	4	1	1	p
								q
4	5	4	4	5	6	3	4	r
11	18	7	12	5	8	2	2	s
6	11	5	7	3	3	2	2	t
7	20	5	15	13	23	8	20	u
1	1	1	1	1	1			v
2	3	2	2	1	2	1	2	w
				2	8	2	8	x
1	1	1	1	4	5	1	1	y
5	5	1	1	2	4			z
132	260	103	168	122	209	64	117	

From the foregoing summary it appears that:

For single letters —

51 pronunciations/ 21 consonants = 2.4 per letter
41 pronunciations/ 5 vowels   = 8.2 per letter
92 pronunciations/ 26 letters   = 3.5 per letter

For simple digraphs —

260 pronunciations/132 digraphs   = 2.0 per digraph

For all other spellings —

209 pronunciations/122 spellings   = 1.7 per spelling

For *all* spellings —

561 pronunciations/280 spellings   = 2.0 per spelling

The classic example of confusion in pronunciations is the nonsense sentence:

Though the rough cough and hiccough plough me through,
    o   ʊf   ɔf   ʊp   aɪ   ɯ

I ought to cross the lough.
   ɔ   ɒk

in which the spelling *ough* is pronounced in 8 different ways. (Since the preceding tables list only spellings of single sounds, only 4 of these pronunciations appear there, but all 8 are pronunciations of *ough*.) Considering only the 8 *ough* words, this sentence may be pronounced by its own analogies in 8^8 or 16,777,216 different ways — only one of which is right!

words may be spelled correctly by 70 phonograms, manipulated according to 26 rules! In between, Hanna *et al.*,[7] in an exhaustive study of English spellings, arbitrarily *assumes* 80% (that is, that a particular phoneme will correspond to a particular grapheme in 80% of the different words in which it occurs) as a criterion of consistent correspondence to the alphabetic principle; and his findings, in terms of phonemes, approximate that figure, *provided* that further factors such as the position of the phoneme in the syllable and the degree of stress are taken into account. When, however, a computer was programmed with an algorithm or rule of procedure, based on the findings of that study, which manipulated 77 graphemes according to 203 rules, it was able to spell just under 50% of the investigated words correctly, and an additional 36% with only one error!

The extraordinary achievements of Dr. Frank C. Laubach in promoting literacy, thru his "each one teach one" technique, in over 300 languages thruout the world are well known. In recent years he has concentrated his efforts on English, using a notation he calls *English the new way*.[8] This admits to 99 symbols, several of them involving a diacritic, the macron, and employs in addition 18 doubled consonants which, while they have phonemically the same signification as the corresponding single consonants, are graphemically additional symbols. These multiple symbolizations of about 40 phonemes provide, for example, a total of 30 symbols for the name-sounds of the 5 vowels, yet *English the new way* describes as "regular" all T.O. spellings within the compass of that notation. Nevertheless, altho in spite of so many alternative spellings it retains the precise T.O. forms of less than 50% of running words, it has recently achieved highly impressive results in teaching English to Chinese students in Hong Kong.

The farthest-out example of such "regularity" is Wijk,[9] who, on the basis of an exhaustive and erudite but highly subjective

[7] Paul R. Hanna *et al.*, *Phoneme-grapheme correspondences as cues to spelling improvement*, Doc. OE-32008 (Washington, D.C.: U.S. Government Printing Office, 1966).

[8] Frank C. Laubach, *English the new way* (Syracuse, N.Y.: New Reader's Press [Box 131, Syracuse, N.Y. 13210]).

[9] Axel Wijk, *Regularized English* (Stockholm: Almquist & Wiksell, 1959).

examination of present-day English orthography, admits to his *Regularized English* 172 graphemes for 50 phonemes (actually only 43 phonemes, since 7 are consonant clusters, not single sounds). Some of the graphemes are used for two or three different phonemes; many are supplemented by considerable lists of exceptions; and the problem of unstressed vowels and diphthongs is treated separately. The result is a notation, easy to *read*, of course, because it retains so many of the familiar irregularities of T.O., but so complex to apply that it would take a linguistic Ph.D. with an encyclopedic memory to *write* it according to specifications. Nevertheless, on the basis that this notation retains the T.O. forms of just over 70% of running words, Wijk implicitly finds T.O. to be 70% "regular."

For more valid answers to our questions, we must begin by defining our terms.

First, is the answer to our question to be stated in terms of whole words or single sounds (phoneme-grapheme correspondences)? Either is legitimate and valuable, but the unit chosen should be clearly stated. The syllable, intermediate in characteristics between the whole word and the single sound, might in theory be used as yet another measure, but, except for professional linguists, who are themselves far from agreement, it is too intangible to warrant consideration for that purpose.

Second, is the answer to be stated in terms of *occurrences* (the frequency with which the phonemically represented unit in question occurs on the average printed page, or in word lists weighted to show relative frequency) or in terms of *items* (the number of different phonemically represented units to be found in the dictionary, or in word lists, whether or not of so-called "commonest" words, *not* weighted to show relative frequency)? For the teaching of *writing*, i.e., spelling, a case can be made for the importance of items. For the teaching of *reading*, data in terms of occurrences are considerably the more important.

Third, are the data derived from connected matter and/or weighted word lists, or from the dictionary or unweighted word lists? From the former sources, both occurrences and items may be determined; from the latter sources, only items.

Finally, assuming as previously stated that a wholly simple phonemic notation will have one and only one symbol for each sound, and one and only one sound for each symbol, how many sounds (phonemes) are to be distinguished, and how strictly is the one-sound, one-symbol standard to be applied to the unstressed short vowels, which in ordinary discourse largely take care of themselves? In other words, by what criterion shall the phonemic or nonphonemic representation of a particular word or sound be determined?

Since the spelling we are seeking to measure is composed wholly of the letters of the Roman alphabet, without diacritics, the criterion against which it is measured must obviously accept the same limitations. To develop the most practicable phonemic notation for English, strictly within the limitations of the existing Roman alphabet, is a far more difficult and complex problem than most people realize.[10] The spelling reform version of World English Spelling (commonly referred to as WES), shown in Table 5, p. 30, is undoubtedly the most thoroly researched such proposal before the public today, with a history of evolution thru international study and conference going back at least 60 years, and in some respects 100 years. In any event, it is the best available touchstone for an answer to our question.

For a "shotgun" answer, in the simplest terms of occurrences of whole words, it suffices to transcribe a representative specimen of connected matter from T.O. into WES and count the proportion of words which retain in WES their T.O. spellings. With the aid, however, of the relative frequency data of my *RF/Sounds* and *RF/Spellings*, more precise and significant answers, especially in terms of occurrences of phonemes, may be obtained.

For a simple answer in terms of words, emphasizing the difference between items and occurrences, Table 3 of *RF/Sounds* lists 1,027 particular words (as distinct from Table 4, root words) which occurred over 10 times in 100,000 words of well-diversified connected matter, and which together made up

[10] See, for example, Appendix C, "Suggested criteria for a phonemic notation for English for general use."

78,633 of the 100,000 words. Of these, the T.O. spellings which are fully phonemic by our WES criterion are:

Unweighted (items): 229 different words out of 1,027 different words, or 22.3% phonemic.

Weighted (occurrences): 36,436 total words out of 78,633 total words, or 46.3% phonemic.

For a recent international conference in London, it was determined, with the help of data on syllables and sounds as well as words, *in RF/Sounds,* that for the entire 100,000 running words investigated, about 40.6% retain their T.O. spellings in the spelling reform version of WES (see Table 9, p. 70).

For a satisfactory answer to the most searching question, the proportion of single sounds which retain their T.O. graphemes in WES, Table 10 of *RF/Spellings* applied the relative frequency data of Table 5 to each and every grapheme of the WES notation, thus giving a precise answer in terms of the 100,000 running words investigated. Table 3, herewith, reproduces the summary of Table 10, showing 74.1% of occurrences and 72.1% of items spelled phonemically in accord with our WES criterion. The final totals of 79.1% occurrences, 79.0% items, refer to the slightly modified version of WES, discussed in Chapter 7 and shown in Table 8, when employed as an initial teaching medium (i.t.m.).

For a final example of employing the WES criterion, without recourse to supplementary data, consider Lincoln's Gettysburg Address, a masterpiece of English literature which includes most of the 41 phonemes in fairly typical proportions. It contains (excluding the title) 267 words, 364 syllables, 958 phonemes (1,149 letters). By our WES criterion, the words, syllables, or phonemes that are fully phonemic are:

106 total words out of 267, or 39.7% phonemic – roughly, 40% of occurrences.

173 syllables out of 364, or 47.5% phonemic – roughly, 50% of occurrences.

712 phonemes out of 958, or 74.3% phonemic – roughly, 75% of occurrences.

In the simplest terms, those are probably the most significant answers to our original question: How phonemic is English spelling?

Table 3 Percent of T.O. phoneme-grapheme correspondences retained by WES

(Summary of Table 10, *RF/Spellings*)

	WES graphemes		Phoneme totals		Percent	
	Oc	It	Oc	It	Oc	It
Consonant subtotals	179,159	32,109	223,526	41,563	79.5	77.3
Vowel subtotals	78,205	14,181	133,545	22,765	58.7	62.2
Consonant and vowel subtotals	257,364	46,290	357,071	64,328	72.2	72.0
Wordsign subtotals	17,756	4	14,620	4		
TOTALS for spelling reform WES	275,120	46,294	371,691	64,332	74.1%	72.1%
Additional percent of T.O. graphemes for i.t.m. WES	18,751	4,451	371,691	64,332	5.0	6.9
TOTALS for i.t.m. WES	293,871	50,745	371,691	64,332	79.1%	79.0%

Chapter 3

Spelling reform: Historical background

As pointed out in Chapter 1, efforts at reforming English spelling were practically coeval with the birth of modern English. It is significant also, in the light of today's emphasis on a phonemic notation—more particularly Pitman's i.t.a.—as an i.t.m., that the two 16th-century reformers cited, like the great majority of their successors, laid chief emphasis on the aspect of facilitating learning to read.

Most of the well-meant efforts of the 17th- and 18th-century spelling reformers need not concern us particularly now. The paralyzing effect of Johnson's dictionary, appearing in 1755, which was an effort not at reform but at standardization, which not merely stopped the clock but even set it back a bit, has already been referred to. Perhaps the most important contribution of this 17th- and 18th-century period, preceding the 19th-century association of shorthand and spelling reform thru Isaac Pitman, was the predominant influence of shorthand in favor of writing by sound rather than by spelling. Here, because the written characters differed completely from the Roman alphabet, there was no visual prejudice in favor of familiar letter combinations, and the obvious advantages of writing phonetically prevailed. Indeed, the very first alphabetic or workable shorthand system, that of John Willis, published anonymously in 1602, expressly stated that "in this Art, not the orthographie, but the sound of the word is respected." [1] The same instructions, in varying form and degree, appear in the great majority of the 210 systems of shorthand

---

[1] Godfrey Dewey, "A sistem of shorthand for general use" (Unpublished doctoral thesis, Harvard University, 1926, with 1960 addendum), pp. 459–460.

published during the next 235 years, prior to Isaac Pitman's Stenographic Soundhand in 1837. As early as 1766, we find Holdsworth and Aldridge taking for granted without argument, in their very definition of shorthand, strict writing by sound, and proceeding to give a clear, full, and essentially accurate account of the minimum 40 sounds recognized from that day to this as essential, and their relations to each other.[2]

With Isaac Pitman, the historical connection between spelling reform and shorthand may be said to have reached its culmination. Thruout his life, Isaac Pitman was active as a militant spelling reformer, and spent the greater part of the large revenue from his shorthand publications on spelling reform experiments and propaganda. As early as 1843 he supplemented his *Fonografic Journal* with the *Fonotipic Journal*, and enunciated the proposition that "As Fonografy becomes the general medium of written communication, Fonotipic printing must follow. . . . We shall, therefore, advocate Fonografy as a means for the attainment of the great need—Fonotipic Printing." Indeed, we are told by Baker: "From this time, he regarded his system of shorthand chiefly as an introduction to spelling reform; and to the advocacy of a phonetic notation, he devoted the strenuous efforts of a lifetime and his own means without stint, while he had also the moral and pecuniary support of a large number of adherents in all parts of the country."[3]

The unceasing efforts by Sir Isaac Pitman, from 1843 until his death in 1897, including his active collaboration with Alexander J. Ellis from 1843 to 1856, are the chief landmark of English spelling reform in Great Britain in the nineteenth century, and his Phonotypy is one of the acknowledged parents of his grandson's i.t.a. Harrison[4] gives an interesting account of his efforts, including Ellis's tribute to him as "the Father of English Phonetic Spelling." It is interesting to note that, in the years following their active collaboration, Ellis moved step by step toward a no-new-letter notation, publish-

---

[2] *Ibid.*, p. 34.
[3] Alfred Baker, *The life of Sir Isaac Pitman* (London: Sir Isaac Pitman & Sons, Ltd., 1913), pp. 83–84.
[4] Maurice Harrison, *Instant reading* (London: Sir Isaac Pitman & Sons, Ltd., 1964), pp. 29–41.

ing in 1870 his *Glossic,* in which "combinations rather than separate letters have definite sounds,"[5] followed in 1880 by his *Dimidium Spelling, or Haaf ov Whot is Needed,*[6] which admitted various alternative spellings in the effort to increase its compatibility with T.O. Glossic may justly be considered as the prototype of the New Spelling (NS) of the Simplified Spelling Society (SSS), which may be regarded as the other parent of i.t.a., since the ligatured symbols of i.t.a. derive almost entirely from the digraphs of New Spelling. No less interesting is the little-known final spelling reform publication of Sir Isaac Pitman, "The Speler," published January 1895, which employed no new letters and almost no diacritics.[7]

In the United States, the first notable effort was Benjamin Franklin's "A Scheme for a New Alphabet and a Reformed Mode of Spelling." Devised in 1768 but not published till 1779, it is best known thru his "Letter to Miss Stevenson," written in 1768 and later published in the Appendix to Noah Webster's "Dissertation on the English Language."[8]

Tauber[9] describes Noah Webster's first meeting with Benjamin Franklin in 1786 and reviews at some length the influence of Webster on American spelling, which, ironically, in view of the tremendous influence of his spelling books, was largely on the side of orthodoxy.

The first serious and sustained effort in the United States was undoubtedly that of Stephen Pearl Andrews, who brought back from London in 1843 some of Isaac Pitman's books and pamphlets on Phonography and Phonotypy, and published in 1844 the first American instruction book on Pitman's Phonography, and in 1846 the *First Book of Andrews and Boyle's Series of Phonotypic Readers.* This was six years before Isaac Pitman's brother, Benn Pitman, removed to America and undoubtedly helped to stimulate the series of teaching experiments in the New England area, later referred to. Andrews' crusading zeal continued thruout a long lifetime, but the con-

---

[5] R. E. Zachrisson, *Anglic* (2d enlarged ed.; Cambridge, England: W. Heffer & Sons, Ltd., 1932), p. 29.
[6] *Ibid.,* pp. 30–31.
[7] *Ibid.,* p. 32.
[8] Tauber, *English spelling reform,* Ch. 3.
[9] *Ibid.*

siderable success of the Andrews and Boyle shorthand publications was not paralleled by the spelling reform aspect.

In 1859 Zalmon Richards, the first president of what is now the National Education Association (NEA), aroused considerable interest by a report of impressive results from teaching reading with a phonetic alphabet, as far back as 1844; and committees were appointed and reported for several years.[10] Other early supporters of spelling reform at the NEA included Horace Mann and President F. A. P. Barnard of Columbia College.

The highwater mark of organized spelling reform in the United States was reached in the dozen years from 1874 to 1886, under the leadership of the American Philological Association (APA). In 1874 the president, Professor Francis A. March of Lafayette College, made a vigorous attack on what he called "the monstrous spelling of the English language" and its impact on education. This was followed up no less vigorously in 1875 by his successor as president, Professor J. Hammond Trumbull of Yale College, which resulted in the formation of a distinguished committee, headed by the first president of the Association, Professor William Dwight Whitney of Yale College, whose report next year, known as the "Principls of '76," reproduced, in the original spelling, in Table 4, has lost nothing of its validity in the ensuing ninety-five years. This was followed, in 1877, by a proposed Standard Fonetic Alfabet[11] so soundly conceived that it served, a generation later, with insignificant alteration of fundamentals, as the basis for the Revised Scientific Alphabet, commonly known as the NEA Alphabet, developed between 1904 and 1911, by joint committees of the American Philological Association, Modern Language Association, and National Education Association, and used as Key 1 of the Funk & Wagnalls New Standard Dictionary. A series of annual reports followed, dealing with various rules and recommendations, culminating in 1886 in a list of some 3,500 amended spellings (involving no new letters), recommended jointly by the Philological Society

[10] *Ibid.*, Ch. 6.
[11] Francis A. March, *The spelling reform* (U.S. Bureau of Education Circular of Information No. 8, 1893 [Washington, D.C.: Government Printing Office, 1893]), pp. 21–22.

Table 4

Principls of '76 °

(1) The true and sole office of alfabetic writing is faithfully and intelligibly to represent spoken speech. So-called "historical" orthografy is only a concession to the weakness of prejudice.

(2) The ideal of an alfabet is that every sound should hav its own unvarying sign, and every sign its own unvarying sound.

(3) An alfabet intended for use by a vast community need not attempt an exhaustiv analysis of the elements of utterance and a representation of the nicest varieties of articulation; it may wel leav room for the unavoidabl play of individual and local pronunciation.

(4) An ideal alfabet would seek to adopt for its characters forms which should suggest the sounds signified, and of which the resemblances should in sum mezure represent the similarities of the sounds. But for general practical use there is no advantage in a system which aims to depict in detail the fysical processes of utterance.

(5) No language has ever had, or is likely to hav, a perfect alfabet, and in changing and amending the mode of writing of a language alredy long writn, regard must necessarily be had to what is practically possibl quite as much as to what is inherently desirabl.

(6) To prepare the way for such a change, the first step is to break down, by the combined influence of enlightened scolars and of practical educators, the immense and stubborn prejudice which regards the establisht modes of spelling almost as constituting the language, as having a sacred character, as in themselvs preferabl to others. All agitation and all definit proposals of reform ar to be welcumd so far as they work in this direction.

(7) An alterd orthografy will be unavoidably offensiv to those who ar first called upon to uze it; but any sensibl and consistent new system wil rapidly win the harty preference of the mass of writers.

(8) The Roman alfabet is so widely and firmly establisht in use among the leading civilized nations that it can not be displaced; in adapting it to improved use for English, the efforts of scolars should be directed towards its use with uniformity and in conformity with other nations.

° American Philological Association committee report, July 1876. Quoted, in original spelling, from Francis A. March, *The spelling reform* (U.S. Bureau of Education Circular of Information No. 8, 1893 [Washington, D.C.: U.S. Government Printing Office, 1893]), p. 12.

of London and the American Philological Association. The classic history of this whole period is that of March,[12] prepared at the request of the United States Commissioner of Education, William T. Harris, and published in 1893.

During this same period, an International Convention for the Amendment of English Orthography was held in Philadelphia in 1876, in conjunction with the Centennial Exposition, with the President of the American Philological Association, Professor S. S. Haldeman of the University of Pennsylvania, presiding and Melvil Dewey as Secretary. The Convention resolved itself into a permanent organization, the Spelling Reform Association (SRA), which elected Francis A. March as President and Melvil Dewey as Secretary, and which commanded the support of a distinguished group of scholars, including many of those active in the APA. During the next decade the SRA supported, supplemented, and encouraged, so far as limited financial resources would permit, the spelling reform efforts of the APA. The chief surviving record of its activities during this early period is found in the bulletins compiled and published by Vickroy[13] in 1881.

In 1887, on the initiative of Dewey, the SRA undertook publication of an official organ, *Spelling*, which recorded and in fact constituted the chief activity of the succeeding period. The difficulties under which it labored are expressed in these few lines from the first editorial:

It is wel known that reformatory jurnals have "no money in them." This jurnal is begun and wil be carried on for a reasonable time, in the hope that the friends of reform and the public wil find it useful, and wil giv a sufficient support. If, after a reasonable time, it is not supported, it wil die; for we reserv the privilege of acknowledging, should occasion arize, the powerful logic of a big printer's bil in a litl tresury. We make no promises and no predictions.[14]

[12] *Ibid.*
[13] T. R. Vickroy (ed.), *Buletins ov the Speling Reform Asoshiashun* (St. Louis, 1881).
[14] *Spelling*, 1, no. 1 (May 1887; Boston: Library Bureau): 7.

Four issues were published during 1887, and five more between 1892 and 1894, before the pressure of Dewey's multifarious activities in the fields of librarianship and higher education, as well as the lack of financial support, resulted in its discontinuance. Largely on my initiative, the publication was revived for a year as a quarterly, in a different format, published jointly by the Simplified Spelling Society (of Great Britain), the Simplified Spelling Board (SSB), and the Spelling Reform Association (SRA), in 1925 and again in 1931, but that story belongs to another era.[15]

Between 1886 and 1906, the chief field of effort shifted to the National Education Association, with the driving force coming increasingly from E. O. Vaile of Chicago, a dedicated, indefatigable, and undiscourageable spelling reformer, albeit handicapped by an irascible disposition. The most important achievements of that period, to which Tauber devotes considerable space,[16] were the adoption in 1898, as an entering wedge, of the famous NEA 12 words,

tho	thru	thoro	program	decalog	pedagog
altho	thruout	thorofare	catalog	demagog	prolog

some of which have since established themselves as preferred usage; and the appointment in 1904, with Vaile as chairman, of the committee which took the lead in developing the Revised Scientific Alphabet (NEA Alphabet), previously referred to. This latter effort was expressly *not* spelling reform, but its proponents rightly believed that adoption of a rational, phonetic notation as a key to prononciation in dictionaries and textbooks would go far toward paving the way for future spelling reform—a parallel, on a less directly influential scale, to the potential effectiveness of i.t.a. as the parent of future spelling reform. Vaile also published[17] a compilation of the most important evidence and arguments of the 19th-century

---

[15] *Spelling*, 1, no. 1 (March 1925); 2, no. 1 (March 1931).

[16] Tauber, *English spelling reform*, Ch. 6.

[17] E. O. Vaile, *Our accursed spelling* (Chicago: Privately printed, 1901 [obtainable from Simpler Spelling Association, Lake Placid Club, N.Y.]).

spelling reform movement, including Max Muller's notable paper, "On Spelling." [18]

The chief event of early 20th-century spelling reform was the formation in 1906 of the Simplified Spelling Board, and its activities during the period that funds were available. Andrew Carnegie had promised $10,000 a year for 10 years to encourage the formation of the Board, and actually gave them $260,000 within 14 years, but the funds were personal subventions, not endowment, and lapsed with his death in 1919; for the Carnegie Corporation, for whatever reasons, refused its support, altho Mr. Carnegie had told Melvil Dewey the last time they met that he considered the movement one of his most worthwhile benefactions. The Board consisted of 50 front-rank scholars and educators, as well as men of letters and men of affairs, with an Advisory Council of some 250 members, also of recognized status or influence in those fields. Its first widely publicized effort was the "List of Common Words Spelled in Two or More Ways," the famous "300 Words" which President Theodore Roosevelt, a member of the Board, directed the public printer to use, and then had to back down under pressure from Congress and confine his usage to White House correspondence. Other lists of recommended words and rules followed, the final dictionary list including some 6,000 words. By means of two or three field workers and a substantial body of publications, including 26 circulars and the Simplified Spelling Bulletin, published quarterly beginning in 1909, the Board enlisted substantial support for a moderate degree of simplification. This included, at one time, 460 universities, colleges, and normal schools, which agreed to use some degree of simpler spellings officially and/or to permit their students to use them; 556 newspapers and periodicals, circulating more than 18 million copies, using the NEA 12 words and most of the 300 words; and some 40,000 individual signers of a postal card pledge to use some degree of simpler spelling in their own writing. The final step of the Board's active period was publication of the

---

[18] *British Fortnightly Review*, April 1876. Reprinted, slightly abridged, in Vaile, *Our accursed spelling.*

1920 *Handbook*,[19] which exhausted the Carnegie funds which had been their chief support. The members of the Board and Council retained their interest and their convictions, but as a group were in no position to provide funds for an active program, so the effect on the public was that the movement had collapsed. Thereafter, the Board continued to operate chiefly on its previously acquired momentum, with occasional unsubsidized meetings to plan and hope.

During this period, partly to avoid confusing the public, the Spelling Reform Association had purposely remained completely inactive. The Board, however, had of necessity, at Mr. Carnegie's insistence, confined its recommendations to limited piecemeal simplifications, eschewing any radical phonetic reform, with or without new letters. When, therefore, the Carnegie support and influence ceased, the most active reformers (mostly members of the Board) reactivated the Spelling Reform Association, in name at least, as a vehicle for more thorogoing reform, and published in 1930 the SRA Fonetic Alfabet, which later became, with very slight alterations, the present SSA (Simpler Spelling Association) phonetic alphabet, shown in Table 6, which thus derives directly from the original 1877 APA Standard Fonetic Alfabet, thru the 1911 NEA Revised Scientific Alphabet, and a further simplification thereof as a key alphabet proposed by the Simplified Spelling Board in 1922.

Meanwhile, in 1908 in Great Britain, the British Simplified Spelling Society (SSS) had been formed with the aid of a modest grant from Mr. Carnegie and with a roster including many of the most distinguished linguistic scholars of Great Britain, and had published in 1910 the first edition of the *Proposals for Simplifying the Spelling of English*,[20] which became in due course the present *New Spelling* [21] of that organization, from which the ligatured characters of i.t.a. chiefly derive. This evolution was substantially furthered by a conference in London in 1930, for which I was chiefly responsible,

[19] Henry Gallup Paine, *Handbook of simplified spelling* (New York: Simplified Spelling Board, 1920).

[20] Harrison, *Instant reading*, pp. 71–73.

[21] Walter Ripman and William Archer, *New Spelling* (6th ed.; London: Sir Isaac Pitman & Sons, Ltd.), 1948.

between representatives of the Simplified Spelling Society and the Anglic Association, founded by Professor R. E. Zachrisson of Uppsala University.[22] The mutually beneficial results of that conference were embodied in due course in the 5th and 6th editions of *New Spelling*, the successor of the original *Proposals,* and received the blessing of the Simplified Spelling Board, which was all that I could offer under the restricted policies still in effect at that time.

The final stage, up till now, of the organized spelling reform movement in this country was the merger in 1946 of the Spelling Reform Association, dating from 1876, and the Simplified Spelling Board, dating from 1906, to form the present Simpler Spelling Association (SSA), with a declared purpose broad enough to include all approaches to the spelling reform problem. The organization's first and most important action was to promulgate, in 1946, World English Spelling (WES), the present form of which is shown in Table 5—a no-new-letter phonemic notation which followed closely the British New Spelling, with only five minor variations, all of which were later ironed out, for the time being, at a conference in London in 1955. This agreement, however, left unchanged in both notations the logical but uncouth /th/ and /dh/ for the unvoiced and voiced sounds of *th*, because none of the conferees could come up with an acceptable alternative. The inclusion of WES in the SSA program at once shifted the emphasis from the two extremes, the piecemeal recommendations of the SSB or the whole-hog phonetic alphabet of the SRA, to the middle ground of substantially phonemic writing with no new letters, toward which both Ellis and Isaac Pitman had moved—the ground consistently occupied by the SSS from the beginning, the ground which offered and offers the greatest possibilities of immediate usefulness.

[22] Zachrisson, *Anglic,* p. 40.

Chapter 4

Spelling reform: Analysis and appraisal

Thruout this study and elsewhere, I have used the term *spelling reform* in its traditional, all-inclusive sense, to denote without distinction all efforts to improve our present spelling of English. This includes not only all proposals based on systematic phonemic codes, whether of the *standardizing* (no-new-letters), *supplementing* (some-new-letters), or *supplanting* (all-new-letters) types, more fully defined and discussed below. It includes also piecemeal or patchwork efforts not based on any complete or consistent phonemic notation or conforming to any clearly defined category. A host of descriptive names have been coined by individual spelling reformers to denote their particular proposals, and generic terms such as simpler spelling, simplified spelling, or alphabet reform have been sometimes employed to distinguish a special type or class of spelling reform, which remains, however, the all-inclusive term.

Phonemic notations and the Roman alphabet

The Roman alphabet is today the most widely used and universally understood medium of communication. With the addition of a few diacritics and a very few additional characters, it is the alphabet of all western European and Scandinavian languages, and in the Eastern world it is the alphabet into which all others are transliterated to achieve international understanding. A recent catalog of the University of New Delhi prints its principal information, in the one catalog, in seven different languages, using five different non-Roman alphabets, but the introduction and supplementary material are

in English in the Roman alphabet; and an official pronounce-
ment of Communist China announces as one of its major educational goals the adoption of the Roman alphabet.[1]

English orthography, which for substantially phonemic
writing should distinguish about 41 sounds, is at present restricted to the 26 letters of the Roman alphabet, 3 of which (*c
q x*) are phonemically duplicates. In consequence, one finds
within the 70,000 words, more or less, of a single abridged
dictionary (exclusive of proper names) some 561 different
spellings of these 41 sounds;[2] a chaos and confusion disas-
trous for elementary education and burdensome thruout adult
life, as well as enormously costly thru the writing and printing
of superfluous letters.

The problem of reducing this confusion to a substantially
one-symbol, one-sound phonemic notation may be approached
in three ways:

Standardizing the Roman alphabet

Standardizing the Roman alphabet by assigning to each
single letter, and to each digraph selected to represent those
sounds for which the available single letters do not suffice, a
single sound. This approach has the immense advantage, for
immediate practical purposes, of providing a substantially
phonemic notation, sufficiently similar to the traditional orthography to be essentially "self-reading" by one who has
never studied the key, which remains strictly within the resources of the universally available Roman alphabet. Because,
however, of the number of consistently used digraphs required, it contributes nothing to reducing the number of
characters to be written or printed.

The World English Spelling (WES) of the Simpler Spelling
Association, shown in Table 5, evolved from the New Spelling of the British Simplified Spelling Society and progres-
sively developed over a period of 60 years by the ablest
specialists on both sides of the Atlantic, comes nearest to
achieving the maximum possibilities of this admittedly cumbersome but immediately practicable solution.

---

[1] Chou En-lai *et al., Reform of the Chinese written language* (Peking: Foreign Language Press, 1965).
[2] See Appendixes A and B, summarized in Tables 1 and 2.

Table 5
World English Spelling
(WES)

Consonants As in		*Vowels and diphthongs* As in
p	pay, happy, cap	**a** at, man; ask; about, data
b	bay, rubber, cab	**aa** alms, father, bah; (ask)
t	town, letter, bit	**ar** army, market, far
d	down, ladder, bid	**e** edge, men, said, head, any
k	keep, week; back; expect; quite	**ae** age, main, say; air
g	game, ragged, bag; exact	**i** it, him, pretty, give; any
f	fast, office, photograph, safe	**ee** each, here, see, be
v	vast, never, save	**o** on, bother, not; was, what
thh	thought, nothing, both	**au** author, law, all, water, ought
th	that, rather, with	**or** order, north, for; story, more
s	seal, lesson, city, race, base	**u** up, other, but, some, touch
z	zeal, puzzle, is, raise, size	**oe** old, note, goes, so, coal, show
sh	shall, pressure, nation, wish	**uu** full, sure, should, good
zh	jabot, pleasure, vision, rouge	**oo** fool, move, group, rule, too
ch	check, church, watch	**ie** ice, tie, kind, might, by
j	just, general, stage, judge	**ou** out, pound, now, bough
m	might, common, them	**oi** oil, point, boy
n	night, dinner, then	**ue** use, your, music, due, few
ng	thing, long, going, single	**er** further, collar, motor, murmur
nk	think, bank, uncle, ankle	**ur** further, her, early, first work
l	late, fellow, deal	
r	rate, married, dear	
w	wet, forward, one, quick	
wh	which, everywhere	
y	yet, beyond, million	
h	had, behind, who	

Separate by a dot successive letters which might otherwise be
read as a digraph —

short.hand, mis.hap, en.gaej, man.kiend

gae.ety, ree.elect, hie.est, loe.er, influu.ens, pou.er, emploi.ee

Linkon'z Getizberg Adres

Forskor and seven yeerz agoe our faatherz braut forthh on this kontinent a nue naeshon, konseevd in liberti, and dedikaeted to the propozishon that aul men ar kreeaeted eekwal.

Nou wee ar en.gaejd in a graet sivil wor, testing whether that naeshon, or eni naeshon soe konseevd and soe dedikaeted, kan long enduer. Wee ar met on a graet batlfeeld ov that wor. Wee hav kum to dedikaet a porshon ov that feeld az a fienal resting-plaes for thoez hoo heer gaev thaer lievz that that naeshon miet liv. It iz aultogether fiting and proper that wee shuud doo this.

But in a larjer sens, wee kanot dedikaet—wee kanot konsekraet—wee kanot haloe—this ground. The braev men, living and ded, hoo strugld heer, hav konsekraeted it far abuv our poor pou.er to ad or detrakt. The wurld wil litl noet nor long remember whot wee sae heer, but it kan never forget whot thae did heer. It iz for us, the living, rather, to bee dedikaeted heer to the unfinisht wurk which thae hoo faut heer hav thus far soe noebli advanst. It iz rather for us to bee heer dedikaeted to the graet task remaening befor us—that from theez onord ded wee taek inkreest devoeshon to that kauz for which thae gaev the last fuul mezher ov devoeshon; that wee heer hieli rezolv that theez ded shal not hav died in vaen; that this naeshon, under God, shal hav a nue burthh ov freedom; and that guvernment ov the peepl, bie the peepl, for the peepl, shal not perish from the urthh.

Such a substantially phonemic no-new-letter code, using digraphs as required to reproduce an essentially self-reading notation, can make an immediate and important educational contribution as an i.t.m. in the earliest grades, or for teaching English as a second language, at the same time that it conditions the next generation to demand or accept a phonemic notation for all reading and writing. Also, for the adult abroad who has been taught English as a second language thru this medium, such a notation offers the exciting possibility of continuing to use it as an international auxiliary medium of communication; *reading* T.O. but continuing to *write* phonemically, thereby bypassing the considerable added burden of acquiring a writing knowledge of our present chaotic English spelling.

Supplementing the Roman alphabet

Supplementing the Roman alphabet by assigning to each of the 23 useful letters a single invariable value and creating some 18 appropriately designed new letters, typographically congruous with the canons of design of the Roman alphabet. If the new letter forms are rightly chosen, such a one-sign, one-sound phonemic notation can be, like the first category, essentially self-reading, even for one who has never studied the key.

A phonemic alphabet of this type, which would save 1 letter in 6 as compared with our present spelling, or about $170 million out of each $1 billion of writing and printing costs,[3] is of course the ideal ultimate solution, but the difficulties of making available the necessary new characters on typewriters and composing machines thruout the world are so great that while such an alphabet can be immediately useful for textbook purposes or dictionary keys, general adoption of this solution probably lies generations in the future. Its exact form at that time can, of course, hardly be predicted now, but at the moment the Simpler Spelling Association (SSA) phonemic alphabet, shown in Table 6, the characters of which were typographically refined by Frederick W. Goudy, the foremost type designer of his generation, comes nearest to meeting the criteria for such a solution.[4]

[3] See *RF/Sounds*, p. 183.
[4] For a fuller discussion of this alphabet, see *RF/Spellings*, Ch. 2.

To the question, Why not just adopt the International Phonetic Association (IPA) alphabet, already widely familiar in somewhat variant forms to linguistic scholars everywhere? there are two answers: its uncouth appearance, and the excessive number of characters which must be written, largely nullifying the enormous savings in writing and printing, on which George Bernard Shaw laid chief emphasis. As employed by Professor Daniel Jones in his *English Pronouncing Dictionary,* for example, that alphabet analyzes 2 of the 24 consonants and 6 of the 17 vowel sounds of the SSA alphabet as diphthongs, and accordingly writes them as digraphs, and writes 4 vowel sounds with a detached diacritic which constitutes an additional character, with the result that it eliminates only 4.65% of the characters required for T.O., as compared with 16.95% for the SSA phonemic alphabet.

Alphabets which depend on diacritics, whether of one form or several, to differentiate the letters of the existing Roman alphabet in order to produce a substantially phonemic notation must be classed as of the supplementing rather than the standardizing type, since for printing, a type or matrix embodying a diacritic is just as much a separate and additional character as a wholly new design, while for the typewriter, unless every letter modified by a diacritic is treated as an individual character, with all the problems that would be involved in providing for a well-designed wholly new character, each letter must be written either with three strokes (letter, back space, diacritic) or if the diacritic(s) be placed on a dead key or keys, two strokes (diacritic, letter). This is still true even if symbols such as " ' _ : / , already somewhere on the standard typewriter keyboard, are employed as the diacritics. Thus, in addition to unsightly appearance and relatively arbitrary significations, alphabets based on diacritics tend to combine the disadvantages of both types.

In summary, a one-sign, one-sound phonemic alphabet, supplying the necessary new characters in harmony with the Roman alphabet, can render immediate practical service as a pronunciation key for dictionaries or textbooks, vastly superior to the illogical mishmash of diacritic-ridden symbols which has long characterized most American dictionaries, but because of the enormous practical difficulties of making the

Table 6   SSA Phonemic Alphabet

Lower case	Capital	Name	As in	Lower case	Capital	Name	As in
24 consonants				*13 vowels*			
p	**p**	*pə*	pin, cup	a	**a**	*ak*	am, pat
b	**b**	*bə*	bin, cub	ɑ	**ɑ**	*a*	alms, part, ma
t	**t**	*tə*	ten, bet	e	**e**	*ek*	edge, let
d	**d**	*də*	den, bed	ɐ	**ɐ**	*a*	age, late, may; **air**
k	**k**	*kə*	come, back	i	**i**	*ik*	is, sit, army
g	**g**	*gə*	gum, bag	ɛ	**ɛ**	*ɛ*	ease, seat, me
f	**f**	*fə*	fan, safe	ɒ	**ɒ**	*ɒk*	odd, not
v	**v**	*və*	van, save	ɔ	**ɔ**	*ɔ*	awed, naught, pshaw
ħ	**ħ**	*ħə*	thigh, bath	ʊ	**ʊ**	*ʊk*	up, ton
ħ	**ħ**	*ħə*	thy, bathe	o	**o**	*o*	open, tone, show
s	**s**	*sə*	seal, race	u	**u**	*uk*	full, should
z	**z**	*zə*	zeal, raise	ɯ	**ɯ**	*ɯ*	fool, shoed, shoe
ʃ	**ʃ**	*ʃə*	assure, rush	ə	**ə**	*ər*	about, murmur, data
ʒ	**ʒ**	*ʒə*	azure, rouge				
ċ	**ċ**	*ċə*	choke, rich	*4 diphthongs*			
j	**j**	*jə*	joke, ridge	ȧ	**ȧ**	*ȧ*	aisle, pint, by
m	**m**	*mə*	met, him	aʊ	**aʊ**	*aʊ*	owl, pound, bough
n	**n**	*nə*	net, thin	ɔ̇	**ɔ̇**	*ɔ̇*	oil, point, boy
ŋ	**ŋ**	*ʊŋ*	ink, thing	iɯ	**iɯ**	*iɯ*	used, pure, due
l	**l**	*lə*	laid, deal				
r	**r**	*rə*	raid, dear	*Supplementary signs*			
w	**w**	*wə*	wet, we	ŧə	**ŧə**	*ŧə*	**the** (wordsign)
y	**y**	*yə*	yet, ye	*	*		*capsign*
h	**h**	*hə*	head, he				

To capitalize a typewritten or longhand word, write the capsign before it.

Phonemic print capitals are heavy or boldface letters, otherwise similar to the small or lower-case letters.

liŋkən'z getizbərg adres

forskor and sevn yɛrz əgo aɪr faħərz brɔt forþ ɒn ħis kɒntinənt ə niu naʃən, kənsɛvd in libərti, and dedikated tu ðə prɒpəziʃən ħat ɔl men ɑr krɛated ɛkwəl.

naɪ wɛ ɑr engajd in ə grat sivil wɔr, testiŋ hweħər ħat naʃən, ɔr eni naʃən so kənsɛvd and so dedikated, kan lɒŋ endiur. wɛ ɑr met ɒn ə grat batl-fɛld ɒv ħat wɔr. wɛ hav kʊm tu dedikat ə porʃən ɒv ħat fɛld az ə fánəl restiŋ-plas fɔr ħoz hu hɛr gav ħar lávz ħat ħat naʃən mát liv. it iz ɔltəgeħər fitiŋ and prɒpər ħat wɛ ʃud duu ħis.

bʊt in ə larjər sens, wɛ kanɒt dedikat — wɛ kanɒt kɒnsikrat — wɛ kanɒt halo — ħis graʊnd. ðə brav men, liviŋ and ded, hu strʊgld hɛr, hav kɒnsikrated it far əbʊv aɪr pʊr paɪər tu ad ɔr ditrakt. ðə wərld wil litl not nɔr lɒŋ rimembər hwɒt wɛ sa hɛr, bʊt it kan nevər fərget hwɒt ħa did hɛr. it iz fɔr ʊs, ðə liviŋ, raħər, tu bɛ dedikated hɛr tu ðə ʊnfiniʃt wərk hwiʧ ħa hu fɔt hɛr hav ħʊs far so nobli ədvanst. it iz raħər fɔr ʊs tu bɛ hɛr dedikated tu ðə grat task rimaniŋ bifor ʊs — ħat frɒm ħɛz ɒnərd ded wɛ tak inkrɛst divoʃən tu ħat kɒz fɔr hwiʧ ħa gav ðə last ful meʒər ɒv divoʃən; ħat wɛ hɛr háli rizɒlv ħat ħɛz ded ʃal nɒt hav dád in van; ħat ħis naʃən, ʊndər gɒd, ʃal hav ə niu bərþ ɒv frɛdəm; and ħat guvərnmənt ɒv ðə pɛpl, bá ðə pɛpl, fɔr ðə pɛpl, ʃal nɒt periʃ frɒm ðə ərþ.

Brief study of the preceding page will enable anyone to read the above selection accurately. A few hours of study will give anyone at all familiar with phonetics a practical working knowledge of this simplest and best phonetic alphabet for English.

new characters everywhere available, such a notation is unlikely to achieve adoption for general use for at least a generation or two.

Supplanting the Roman alphabet

Supplanting the Roman alphabet by creating and making
available on typewriters and composing machines thruout the
world at least 41 wholly new characters—the solution advocated by Shaw for his Proposed British Alphabet [5]—is a fantastic proposal which is, from a practical standpoint, completely
unrealistic. Since the whole purpose of writing or printing is
to be read, and since, for the person who had not mastered the
key, such a notation would be a completely unintelligible
cipher, it is quite inconceivable that any writer or publisher
would deliberately so obstruct communication with his desired readership.[6] Even a dictator with power to reform English spelling by decree, as Kemal Ataturk reformed Turkish—
in that case, by *adopting* the Roman alphabet—would hesitate
to cut his country off from facile communication with the rest
of the world by enforcing a notation wholly unknown outside
his own jurisdiction. It would seem, therefore, as if Shaw's
declared purpose for his Proposed British Alphabet, to "use
it side by side with the present lettering until the better ousts
the worse," must have been written with tongue in cheek.

In the preface to Wilson's *The miraculous birth of language*
already cited, Shaw, who used a simple form of Pitman Shorthand for many years for most of his writing, and was therefore fully conscious of the immense values of shorthand for
personal use, was equally unrealistic in his conception of his
Proposed British Alphabet, for he describes at some length
the characters of Sweet's Current Shorthand as indicating the
type of character he had in mind for writing *and printing.* The
idea of substituting shorthand characters for the Roman alphabet for printing goes back at least as far as Isaac Pitman's *Sten-*

---

[5] See, particularly, Shaw's preface to Richard Albert Wilson, *The miraculous
birth of language* (London: J. M. Dent & Sons Ltd., 1941), pp. ix–xxxvii,
esp. pp. xxx–xxxv.

[6] For the alphabet adopted by the Public Trustee in fulfilment of Shaw's
direction, see the Shaw Alphabet edition of *Androcles and the lion* (Baltimore: Penguin Books, Inc., 1962).

ographic Soundhand in 1837, and insofar as it would at one stroke substitute phonemic writing for the chaos of T.O., it has a distinct appeal. Unfortunately, however, there is an inherent and inescapable contradiction between the requirements of shorthand and print, in that one must be appraised primarily in terms of the hand, the other in terms of the eye.

The characters of a page of print are set up once and read perhaps a thousand, perhaps a million times, and the longest character, such as *m*, takes no longer to set than the simplest character, such as *o*. The requirements of letter form should therefore be determined solely by the greatest possible distinctiveness of form or minimum of effort for the eye. A page of shorthand, on the contrary, is written once and read, in general, but once or twice; the writing being the process involving enormously the greater effort, and the one into which the time element chiefly enters. The paramount consideration should be, therefore, to minimize the effort for the hand, preserving only such distinctiveness of form as shall be readily and unmistakably perceptible to the eye. Since coincidence between the forms of minimum manual effort and maximum visual distinction is quite inconceivable, any attempt to combine the two, as called for by Shaw's specifications, must of necessity fall far short of the best forms for either, considered separately. Also, like any other notation of the *supplanting* category, it lacks the essentially self-reading quality attainable with either the *standardizing* or *supplementing* category, without which no solution can hope to be translated from theory into practice.

For *handwriting*, as distinct from typing or printing, a very strong case can be made, for the reasons just given, for characters completely divorced from the letter forms of the traditional Roman alphabet. Such characters, integrated into a simple, legible phonemic system of shorthand for general use, have enormous possibilities of usefulness; not merely for notetaking or for personal correspondence with other writers of the system, but much more in saving the time and effort of the author, considered merely as a manual laborer—the aspect Shaw repeatedly emphasized—and most of all, perhaps, by providing the creative writer with the ability to keep pace with his own thoughts, which all too often come too fast for the sluggish longhand pen and, outrunning the record, are lost at the time, perhaps forever.[7]

Phonemic notations which, *for printing and typing,* completely reject the Roman alphabet, whether in favor of shorthand-type characters or no, are an interesting subject for philosophic speculation, but, cutting loose from the rest of the world and lacking the essentially self-reading quality indispensable to any gradual or voluntary introduction, are likely to remain in the realm of philosophic speculation.

Piecemeal and patchwork proposals

In addition to efforts to provide a substantially phonemic alphabet for English, there have been many proposals for *piecemeal* or step-by-step improvement, consisting usually of some combination of rules and lists. Two of the most noteworthy have been the list of about 3,500 words, based on 24 joint rules (actually 10 rules and 14 lists of words) promulgated by the Philological Society of England and the American Philological Association in 1886,[8] and the final list of about 6,000 words, based on 28 rules (actually 27 rules and a short special list) published by the Simplified Spelling Board in 1920 [9] – in neither case based on any complete or consistent phonemic notation.

I have used the term "patchwork proposals" for those schemes which involve elements of more than one of the categories above described, which must always be classed with the more radical component since they necessarily accept its disadvantages, and for the hundreds of schemes devised, and insistently advocated as the one thing needful to achieve the goal, by well-meaning, deeply concerned amateurs whose zeal outruns their linguistic scholarship, as well as by more competent linguists insufficiently aware of the intricate interrelations of the decisions involved, summarized in Appendix C, "Suggested criteria for a phonemic notation for English for general use."

---

[7] For a fuller discussion of the potential values of shorthand for general personal use, see my unpublished doctoral thesis, "A sistem of shorthand for general use," esp. pp. x–xi and 9–21.

[8] March, *The spelling reform,* pp. 63–86.

[9] Paine, *Handbook of simplified spelling,* Part 3.

Advantages and objections

The principal arguments in favor of spelling reform fall into three main categories:

1. Economy of time and effort and money now wasted in the writing and printing of superfluous letters. This has already been pointed out earlier in this chapter. In terms of social and economic values, I regard this, in spite of Shaw's emphasis, as the least of the three. For one thing, it applies only to the supplementing one-sign, one-sound type of reform, which for reasons already pointed out has little or no prospect of coming into general use in our time. The more immediately practicable standardizing, no-new-letter type actually effects no significant saving in letters, since the systematically used digraphs just about offset the elimination of superfluous letters.

2. Facilitating the already rapid spread of English as the dominant international auxiliary language, or second language of the world—a destiny for which it is preeminently fitted except for its intricate and disordered spelling. This aspect will be more fully discussed in Chapter 7.

3. The effect on elementary education, and thru education on school dropouts and juvenile delinquency, adult illiteracy and unemployability, and on the human misery as well as social and economic evils which these involve. This is at once the most urgent need and the greatest opportunity for spelling reform, for use of a phonemic notation such as i.t.a. or WES can make an immediate and important educational contribution toward mitigating the impact of T.O. on the present generation of children, at the same time that it conditions them, as the adults of the next generation, to demand or accept a phonemic spelling reform. This aspect is discussed at length in Chapters 5 and 6.

Most of the hoary arguments against spelling reform—loss of etymologies, confusion of homonyms (more accurately, homophones), necessity for reprinting existing books, lack of a standard of pronunciation, etc.—current in the 19th century but rarely heard today—have been minutely analyzed and rejected by the most competent philologists and linguists before most of us were born. For those interested they will be found, with appropriate comments and quotations, in Appendix D.

The real obstacles, which in my judgment effectively preclude any hope of changing the spelling habits of the present adult generation, include:

1. Unawareness, by most of those who have learned to spell (passably, at least), of how heavily the burden of T.O. bears on today's school child.

2. An almost total lack of awareness, even by fully literate adults, of the number and nature of the sounds of their own language.

3. Total lack of experience (except for shorthand writers) in writing English phonemically in any notation.

4. Lack of agreement among reformers as to exact details of a notation sufficiently compatible with T.O. to bridge the necessary transition period of use concurrently with T.O.

5. Unavoidable distraction from the substance of any written communication to its form, during the transition period.

6. Overshadowing and reinforcing all the rest, the inertia which dreads the effort of the change.

It should be obvious how largely most of these difficulties would be resolved for a generation which had arrived at its competence in T.O. thru employment of a phonemic notation as an i.t.m.

Chapter 5

Roadblocks, and some attempted detours

The paramount importance of the reading problem is sufficiently evidenced by the phenomenal growth of the International Reading Association since its formation in 1955, and the enormous proportion of current educational literature devoted to the topic. The *Encyclopedia of Educational Research* states, as of 1960, "One hundred or more studies are now being published yearly," [1] and takes 151 pages to report on reading research as against only 2 to 5 pages each for most of the other school subjects; and Chall refers categorically, as of 1967, to "more than one thousand reading research studies completed each year." [2]

Even a cursory inspection of this vast volume of research and discussion reveals how large a proportion is concerned either with the teaching of spelling or, more broadly, with the problems created by the irregularities of English spelling. Such investigations are dealing chiefly with symptoms, not with the disease, and resemble nothing so much as efforts to build a modern emergency hospital at a grade crossing instead of eliminating the crossing. Indeed, the various reading methods which have battled each other so fiercely, with varying fortunes, over the past century are revealed as chiefly efforts to rationalize the irrational; to sweep the difficulties of English spelling under the rug, where they bulk too large to be disposed of in so summary a fashion.

[1] Chester W. Harris (ed.), *Encyclopedia of Educational Research* (3d ed.; New York: The Macmillan Company for the American Educational Research Association, 1960).

[2] Jeanne S. Chall, *Learning to read: The great debate* (New York: McGraw-Hill Book Company, 1967), p. 313.

To one who has read thus far, even without the exhaustive analysis of T.O. presented in *RF/Spellings,* it should hardly be necessary to labor the point that the currently accepted spellings of T.O. are the chief roadblock to learning to read and write, the cause of the enormous traffic jam of conflicting theories about how to evade the issues posed by the built-in irregularities of T.O. Past history, contemporary analogies, and common sense unite in emphasizing this point.

Past history reveals that recognition of the difficulties of English spelling goes back more than six centuries to Chaucer; that efforts at spelling reform have been specifically coupled to making learning to read easier for at least 400 years, going back to Hart and Bullokar, cited in Chapter 1; and that the great majority of spelling reformers since that time, whether or not they looked on their proposals as transition alphabets or as immediate reforms to be adopted forthwith by everyone, including the current generation of adults, have made better learning to read and write their primary objective.

Arguing from contemporary analogies, it would appear that world languages such as Italian or Spanish, the spelling of which is substantially phonemic, have no such problems, either in theory or practice, as does English, but in general teach beginning reading by some form of what we would call a simple phonic method—learning the phonemic values of the letters and proceeding to read and write without further ceremony. Particularly instructive is the example of Wales, where the elementary schools are bilingual, and, as reported by Harrison,[3] English is taught by a variety of methods, with the look-and-say or sentence methods predominating, and encountering the usual difficulties, but Welsh, which, believe it or not, is by its own code spelled phonemically, is invariably taught, usually by the same teachers to the same pupils, by a simple phonic method as a matter of course.

From a common-sense standpoint, stripped of the sophistications of educational theorizing or rationalizations, it should be sufficiently obvious that a putatively alphabetic spelling embodying the characteristics summarized in Chaper 2 and

---

[3] Harrison, *Instant reading,* pp. 76–78. See also Harrison, "The use of simplified spelling in teaching infants to read and write" (Simplified Spelling Society Pamphlet No. 9 [London: Sir Isaac Pitman & Sons, Ltd., 1946]).

analyzed at length in *RF/Spellings*, presents an enormous roadblock in the path to reading and writing when encountered for the first time by the little child to whom the very idea of written symbols corresponding to spoken sounds is a novelty. Most reading methods are essentially efforts to detour that roadblock, to put off facing the hard facts of T.O. as long as possible.

Chall based her recent massive study of the problem, *Learning to read: The great debate,* on visits to several hundred classrooms and interviews with hundreds of schoolmen, analysis of the vast body of existing research on beginning reading, detailed study of basal reading series in widespread use, including interviews with their authors and editors, and exploration of the several factors influencing the practice of beginning reading instruction. She classes existing methods broadly as meaning-emphasis and code-emphasis, and in the first and perhaps most important of her conclusions expresses a qualified judgment that "a code-emphasis method . . . produces better results, at least up to the point where sufficient evidence seems to be available, the end of the third grade." [4] Unfortunately she does not sufficiently bring out the important point, repeatedly and correctly emphasized by Pitman, that use of a phonemic notation (in his case, i.t.a.) for the first teaching of reading is not a *method* but a *medium,* applicable, to good advantage, to *any* method.[5] Of this, more hereafter.

Applying loosely, in general terms, Chall's categories of code-emphasis and meaning-emphasis, it is perhaps fair to say that the 19th century was dominated by code-emphasis, the first half of the 20th century by meaning-emphasis, with a somewhat new emphasis on medium rather than method emerging today. It is a far cry, indeed, from the *New England Primer* and the *McGuffey Readers,* which successfully educated a substantial proportion of our ancestors, to the multi-million-dollar basal reading series which have dominated the situation in recent years. What characteristics of the roadblock have influenced the various detours which have brought us to where we are today?

Consider first the detours which the English spelling road-

---

[4] Chall, *Learning to read,* p. 307.
[5] Pitman and St. John, *Alphabets and reading,* p. 117.

block has evoked for the code-emphasis methods, loosely grouped under the term "phonics." The basic principle which characterizes the phonics group is to learn the sounds of the letters (the code) and then proceed to combine them into words and sentences. Were English as phonemically spelled as, say, Italian, the problems would be relatively simple: the order of introduction of the letters during the relatively brief period of learning the code; the choice of words for reading and writing appropriately related to the substantial hearing and speaking vocabulary which the child already possesses; and the selection of subject matter of interest and literary value as well as relevance to the child's interests and experience. Instead, in English, the teacher or textbook author is immediately confronted by questions such as these:

1. What are "the sounds of the letters"? The letter *a* is used by itself (disregarding its use in simple digraphs such as *ea*, or more complex combinations) as a grapheme for 8 different phonemes, the most frequent grapheme for 4 of these (as in h*a*d *a*bout m*a*king *a*ll), and the same is true of the letter *o* (as in *o*f d*o* n*o* f*o*r); *u* for 8, *e* for 6, and *i* for 5 phonemes; a total of 35 uses of the 5 vowel letters as single letter graphemes.[6]

2. On what basis shall graphemes, or phonemes, be selected for introduction: frequency of occurrence or freedom from ambiguity or some other?

3. To what extent should "sight words" be introduced to facilitate early presentation of "meaningful" (save the mark!) connected matter without coming to grips with those markedly irregular spellings which are especially common among the short and simple words of high frequency?

4. Shall the alphabet be taught by rote, with the familiar letter names, as a first step; at a considerably later stage, when the "code" has become somewhat familiar; or as a final step because of its indispensability for consulting alphabetically arranged lists such as the dictionary, library catalog, phone book, etc.?

[6] Dewey, *RF/Spellings*. Derived from Tables 5 and 6 (see also Ch. 6). Note that these examples are taken from those actually encountered in the 100,000 running words, composed of about 10,000 different words, investigated and reported on in *RF/Spellings*, which total less than two-thirds of the examples found in one abridged dictionary and reported here in Appendixes A and B.

5. If the alphabetic names be taught early, how shall graphemes be referred to in teaching: by letter names or by sounds, with at least a neutral vowel sound accompanying the consonants and perhaps a consonant background for the vowels, especially the short vowels? "C-A-T spells CAT" is often used as a symbol of simplicity, yet if the child spells it aloud by rote, using the letter names, /sɛ-a-tɛ/ (WES, /see-ae-tee/), he has uttered only 1 of the 3 sounds of the word; while if he spells *which,* /dʊbl yu-aċ-ȧ-sɛ-aċ/ (WES, /dubl yoo-aech-ie-see-aech/), he has again uttered only 1 of its 4 sounds, and that one in the wrong context!

Considering only these 5 limitations on freedom of choice, it is obvious that their permutations and combinations offer almost endless scope for differences in professedly phonic methods, and that altho the advocates of phonics repudiate the principle of a controlled vocabulary as one of the most serious faults of most meaning-emphasis methods, the various choices which must be made by code-emphasis methods inevitably result in a substantial restriction of vocabulary over a considerable, altho much shorter, period. At best, the phonics methods involve a somewhat tortuous maze of detours around obstacles in order to delay the final confrontation with the full facts of T.O.

Since the main objective of the Reading Reform Foundation, organized in 1961, might be summarized in three words as "back to phonics," it is pertinent to point out that had the code-emphasis phonics methods proved sufficiently satisfactory, the meaning-emphasis look-and-say methods against which their sharpest invectives are hurled could never have achieved their present predominance.

Consider now some of the detours around the English spelling roadblock attempted by the meaning-emphasis methods — variously referred to as "whole word," "look-say," "sight word," "sentence method," "reading for meaning," and other more-or-less descriptive terms — which find their apotheosis in the enormously overelaborated basal reading series of today, with their severely controlled vocabularies. These offer the pupil, in the early years, a reading and writing vocabulary of only hundreds of words as against the thousands of words which are already well within his comprehension as a part of his hearing and speaking vocabulary. By the device of suppressing as long as possible the basic fact that written English is, in principle, an alphabetic system consisting of graphemes purporting to represent phonemes, they postpone even farther than the code-emphasis methods the necessity for dealing with the difficulties, variously detoured by both types, which must eventually be encountered on the road to the cold, hard facts of T.O. Meantime, however, the severe restriction of vocabulary imposes an enormous obstacle to development of creative writing in the earliest grades, a factor which will be discussed later under the positive approach to the problem.

Among the more fantastic devices or rationalizations evolved to justify prolonged reliance on nonalphabetic recognition of word wholes is dependence on the shape, that is, the length or, more particularly, the configuration of the word image — carried sometimes even to the point of teaching the child to draw block outlines around the ascenders or descenders. Table 7 may perhaps serve, without discussion, as a reductio ad absurdum for this particular detour from common sense. The consequences of reliance on such expedients have been trenchantly expressed by Lowe, herself a highly successful remedial teacher:

What children know as reading is a difficult, tedious, complicated, confusing, time-consuming, uninteresting, and unserviceable exercise in visual recall, association, surmise, invention, prediction, paraphrase, substitution, and interpolation or omission at will — all blighted by an incessant striving for speed. This uncoordinated exertion mutilates or even obliterates the meaning of the writer. Communication between mind and mind is not even glimpsed as a goal, since the reader decides, instead of discovering, what this meaning may be.

The essence of the matter is not that reading has not been taught, altho indeed it has not, but that something has been taught which is not reading. Imposed upon the majority of the students of high school and college age today is a perverse and illogical concept of a word as a visual symbol of meaning instead of as a symbol, by grace

Table 7   The case against relying on length and/or configuration as an aid to word recognition

Length

A spot check of the main entries in one abridged dictionary (the *American College Dictionary*, 1953) indicates the approximate number of words of each length (on a word list, not a running words basis) to be as follows:

Letters	2	3	4	5	6	7	8	9	10	Over 10
Words	710	1,930	7,820	5,280	10,450	11,680	10,660	6,290	5,680	4,870

What price length as a distinguishing characteristic of a word?

Configuration

The lower-case Roman letters are of three heights:

Middles:	a	c	e	i	m	n	o	r	s	u	v	w	x	z	(14)
Ascenders:	b	d	f	h	k	l	t								(7)
Descenders:	g	j	p	q	y										(5)

The possible profiles (configurations) of these, in combination (without allowing for nonorthographic sequences), are:

For 2-letter words, 3^2, or 9

Configuration	xx	x xx	x xx	xx xx	xx x	xx x	xx xx	x xx x	x xx x	(9)
Example	in	it	to		my	go		by		(6)

For 3-letter words, 3^3, or 27

Configuration	xxx	x xxx	x xxx	xx xxx	xxx x	xxx x	xxx xx	x xxx x	x xxx x	(9)
Example	can	and	who	all	any	age	spy	sky	ugh	(9)

Configuration	xxx xxx	xx xxx	x x xxx	x xxx	xx xxx x	x x xxx x	x xxx xx	x xxx x	x xxx x	(9)
Example		the	but	how	fly			buy	dye	(6)

Configuration	xxx xxx	xxx xx	xxx x x	xxx x	x xxx xx	x xxx x x	xx xxx x	x xxx x	x xxx x	(9)
Example	gyp	pyx	pay	you		ply		yet	phi	(7)

$$\underline{27} \qquad \underline{22}$$

For 4-letter words (the mean length on a running words basis), 3^4, or 81

For 7-letter words (the median length on a dictionary basis), 3^7, or 2,187

For the first configuration of 3-letter words (xxx), there are at least 92 examples; 9 of them among the 100 commonest words, 10 more among the 1,000 commonest.

What price configuration as a distinguishing characteristic of a word?

of the letters which compose it, of the sound which conveys the meaning.[7]

As with the code-emphasis methods, the number of different expedients employed by the meaning-emphasis methods to detour the T.O. roadblock, plus such alternatives as silent or oral reading, the relation of instruction in reading to instruction in writing, programmed learning, etc., together with their variations in sequence and in degree of emphasis, are quite sufficient to offer a considerable variety of approaches. All, however, share the basic defects of limitation of vocabulary, deferred recognition of the alphabetic principle, and prolonged exposure to the inanities of the "Dick and Jane" type of material instead of subject matter of intrinsic interest and literary value; and all, like the code-emphasis methods, must eventually come to grips with T.O. as it is.

It should be evident by now that the chief roadblock to learning to read and write English, as compared with other world languages, lies in the complex irregularities of the T.O. code. Soffietti, in a brilliantly clear and penetrating scholarly article: (1) presents the linguist's concept of language, speech, and meaning; (2) discusses the problems of reading and writing, including the contrast between the phonemes of Italian and their spellings, and the phonemes of English and their spellings; (3) outlines an approach to reading instruction based in large part on the suggestions of Bloomfield; [8] and (4) finally summarizes the whole in these words: "This approach to reading and writing instruction is not going to eliminate reading and writing as a problem in American education. There is only one radical solution for this: a spelling reform." [9]

Quite obviously Soffietti, like many others, regards the ultimate spelling reform solution as belonging to a future too unpredictably remote to be taken into account today. Fortunately there is an alternative solution, based on the *medium*

---

[7] Helen R. Lowe, "Solomon or salami," *The Atlantic Monthly,* 204, no. 5 (November 1959): 128–131.

[8] Leonard Bloomfield, "Linguistics and reading," *Elementary English Review,* 19: 125–130, 183–186.

[9] James P. Soffietti, "Why children fail to read: A linguistic analysis," *Harvard Educational Review,* 25, no. 2: 63–84.

of instruction, not the *method,* which provides for the present a relatively well-paved detour, and could in time lead to dismantling the roadblock itself—use of a phonemic notation as an i.t.m., to be followed in due course, for the present generation, by a phased transition to reading and writing T.O. in its presently acceptable form.

A phonemic notation as an initial teaching medium

Most methods, of whatever type, take for granted as a matter of course that the medium of instruction for beginning reading and writing is T.O. The idea that children might learn two alphabets more easily than one, especially when the goal is mastery of the second, does not, at first thought, commend itself to common sense. Nevertheless, evidence has been accumulating for more than a century that normal, native English-speaking children, at least, can be taught to read and write using *only* a substantially phonemic notation until they have acquired a considerable degree of fluency, and thereafter make a complete transition to T.O., in substantially less time than by any established method using T.O. only, and with markedly superior results, judged strictly by current conventional tests and standards.

Harrison [10] cites a number of favorable reports on experiments in Great Britain during the 1840s and 1850s using Fonotypy (Phonotypy), the alphabet devised by Isaac Pitman and A. J. Ellis, and reports at some length on a series of 16 experiments in British schools in England and Scotland, between 1915 and 1924, using a no-new-letter phonemic notation not unlike the later British New Spelling, or WES, but with incredibly limited teaching materials; nevertheless, the use of this notation, as reported by the teachers and headmasters or headmistresses, yielded impressively favorable results. [11] Zachrisson [12] quotes from the publications of Pitman, and Ellis reports of successful experiments in the 1840s which undoubt-

[10] Harrison, *Instant reading,* pp. 34–36.
[11] *Ibid.,* pp. 58–60. See also "The best method of teaching children to read and write" (Simplified Spelling Society Pamphlet No. 7 [London: Sir Isaac Pitman & Sons, Ltd., 1942]).
[12] Zachrisson, *Anglic,* p. 27.

edly influenced his own well-thought-out system, Anglic, which in turn influenced the development of New Spelling in the 1930s, as recorded in Chapter 3.

In the United States the 1840s and 1850s witnessed a number of experiments, chiefly in the New England area. As previously mentioned, Zalmon Richards, first president of the NEA, reported to them that he had taught reading with a phonetic alphabet in one-fourth the time usually required.[13] Experiments in and around Boston achieved results which in 1851 elicited from Horace Mann a striking testimonial quoted by Ellis:

> Dear Sir:
>
> Having witnessed the exercises of a class of nine children under your care in reading phonography (or phonetic shorthand) and phonotypy (or phonetic print) it gives me pleasure to assure you of the delight which their performance gave me. I think the nine Muses were never listened to by a more grateful audience . . . The children you exhibited had certainly made most wonderful proficiency, and were, in several of the essentials of good enunciation and reading, *years* in advance of most children who had been taught in the old way.
>
> Yours truly
> Horace Mann [14]

A recent study by Bothe[15] deals with 6 of the most important 19th century experiments. The first 3—Waltham, Massachusetts, 1852–1860; Cincinnati, Ohio, 1851–1858; and Syracuse, New York, 1853–1863—employed the Pitman-Ellis Phonotypy, which had been brought to this country by Stephen Pearl Andrews in 1843 and by Benn Pitman in 1852. The latter 3—St. Louis, Missouri, 1866–1892; Boston, Massachusetts, 1866–1879; and Portland, Maine, 1875–1883—employed

---

[13] Tauber, *English spelling reform*, Ch. 6.

[14] A. J. Ellis, *The American phonetic dictionary of the English language* (Cincinnati: Longley Bros., 1855), "General introduction," pp. xxxiv–xxxv.

[15] Albert E. Bothe, Jr., *Nineteenth-century experiments with transitional reading media* (Baltimore: Dept. of Education, Johns Hopkins University, 1967).

Edwin Leigh's Pronouncing Orthography, which, owing to the complexity as well as number of its 70 characters, which obviously provided numerous alternative symbolizations, must be regarded as only a reading, not a writing, medium.

Particular interest attaches to the Waltham experiment, not only for its priority but also because the moving spirit behind it was undoubtedly the Rev. Thomas Hill, later president of Harvard University, who was chairman of the Waltham School Committee at the time that the project was undertaken. Particular interest attaches also to the St. Louis experiment because of its long duration, 26 years, and because William T. Harris, who was Superintendent of Schools in St. Louis during the first 14 years of the experiment, went on to become U.S. Commissioner of Education, and singled out that particular experiment for attention in his letter of transmittal of the March report.[16]

In view of the uniformly impressive successes reported from so many experiments, going back more than a century both in the United States and in Great Britain, it is pertinent to ask why none of these projects survived and took root. For one familiar with the problems of introducing an educational specialty, especially a revolutionary specialty, into the schools, the answers are not hard to find. For this particular revolution, a phonemic notation as an i.t.m., here are some of the more important:

1. The inherent prima facie unreasonableness of the basic idea that to teach a child two complete systems of reading and writing — first one he will not continue to use and then the one he must use thereafter — will give better results more quickly than to teach the one he must continue to use in the first place.

2. The natural fear that the transition to T.O. might prove confusing or ineffective, a fear which dies hard, even today, tho by now it should certainly be moribund.

3. Lack of standardized tests and objective measurements to back up subjective and therefore controversial judgments.

4. Defects and deficiencies of the various media employed, which in most cases fell far short of the compatibility of i.t.a.

5. Lack of a supply of teachers adequately familiar with the phonemic facts of English, or means for training such teachers,

[16] March, *The spelling reform*, pp. 7–8.

once the original protagonist of each project dropped out of the picture.

6. Paucity of teaching materials, costly and difficult for any publisher to produce for a limited and highly problematic market. Only a strong publisher, moved by conviction as well as the tenuous hope of ultimate profit, could have hoped to take on and overcome successfully all the other obstacles involved.

7. The dead-weight pressure of conformity, which called for stark courage as well as flaming conviction for a school board or principal to shoulder the overcoming of the foregoing obstacles instead of continuing in the safe, well-trodden paths.

8. Finally, last but by no means least, the active hostility of vested interests, intellectual as well as financial—a phenomenon by no means confined to the 19th century. The motivation of a commercial publisher who sees his market for a highly profitable textbook series—representing a considerable investment—threatened is sufficiently obvious, and we are all familiar with brass-knuckle tactics in that field. There is also, however, a more poignant intellectual vested interest, that of the educator-author who has developed his whole educational philosophy on the major premise that the subject matter of elementary reading and writing is traditionally spelled English, and has perhaps authored a successful reading series based on one or another of the various "emergency hospital" techniques. The shock of having the rug pulled from under his major premise, thereby largely invalidating much of the superstructure, is not conducive to dispassionate educational statesmanship, and when it touches the pocket nerve as well, via diminished royalties, the results in too many cases are all too predictable.

Against such handicaps, the astonishing aspect is not that those earlier efforts did not survive and succeed in establishing a beachhead for phonemic notations as initial teaching media, but that the driving force of their champions succeeded so well while it was applied.

Bothe accepts the foregoing 8 reasons, which were published before his study was completed, as disposing of any generalized conclusion that discontinuance of the 6 experiments he investigated was due to lack of effectiveness.[17] With

---

[17] Bothe, *Nineteenth-century experiments*, p. 117.

regard to specific cases where he suggests that unsatisfactory results may have been a factor, it seems fair to emphasize that the conditions referred to under points 4, 6, and 3 are quite different today, and that point 8 is exacerbated both by the multimillion-dollar investments of publishers in basal reading series, and by the hostages to fortune given by much of the pontificating of educators, which falls flat once the practicability of a phonemic notation as an i.t.m. is demonstrated.

There are, of course, detours other than a straightforward phonemic alphabet, which concern themselves primarily with the medium rather than the method, altho these are usually more applicable to the code-emphasis type. Fry, for example, has devised an ingenious diacritical marking system,[18] which, at the cost of numerous extra strokes, may be written on any standard typewriter. (The demerits of diacritic notations in general have already been commented on in Chapter 4.) The system of Caleb Gattegno, described in his *Words in color,*[19] which uses 47 different colors, represents the latest and most elaborate use of color as a diacritic to differentiate the multiple significations of the letters of the T.O. code, but, while it is undoubtedly effective as an aid to reading, it is as unusable for the correlative process of writing as were the 70 complex characters of Leigh's Pronouncing Orthography.[20] The possibilities of such detours, separately or in combination, are almost endless, but they remain just that: attempts to detour the recognized roadblocks of T.O. instead of trying to undermine and eventually remove them — in other words, "emergency hospital" techniques.

i.t.a.

Specific examination and discussion of i.t.a., as the outstanding exemplar of the i.t.m. technique today, will be deferred to the next chapter. Since, however, a favorite gambit of opponents of i.t.a. is to extrapolate from the consistent record of discontinuances of the i.t.m. technique reported above, it seems pertinent to put on record at this point some of

[18] Edward Fry, "A diacritical marking system to aid beginning reading instruction," *Elementary English,* 41, no. 5 (May 1964).

[19] New York: Xerox Corporation, 1968.

[20] *Vide supra,* pp. 50–51.

the factors that i.t.a. has going for it which were lacking in the past:

1. A leader of genius, integrity, and immense energy, Sir James Pitman, who combined for the first time three indispensable attributes: a dedicated and technically competent understanding of the problem, hereditary as well as acquired; command of substantial publishing resources; and high-level contacts sufficient to persuade the establishment to sanction the crucial first step, adequate experimentation in the schools under unimpeachable auspices.

2. Sir James's insistence on the sole purpose of better teaching of reading and writing; expressly disavowing the traditional, as well as family and personal, link to spelling reform.

3. A markedly superior medium, combining several important characteristics: a structure shaped to the express purpose of an i.t.m., rather than as a spelling reform notation; a time-tested phonemic basis, derived from Pitman and Ellis and from New Spelling, as well as from the century and a quarter experience of Pitman Shorthand; skilfully selected concessions from strictly phonemic writing (a more important factor than most people realize) to achieve maximum compatibility with T.O. in the interest of minimum effort of transition; restriction to one lower-case alphabet; and design of the additional new characters to retain or, so far as practicable, suggest the more familiar T.O. spellings of each phoneme, and preserve the "top coastline" of T.O.

4. A more favorable educational climate, accustomed to standardized tests and objective measurements, in which valid research can command immediate attention and respect—a climate more hospitable to change in the established order.

5. Assured financial support for the beginning, as a venture of faith, from the Pitman publishing interests and from Sir James himself, and at one point from the British Ministry of Education, supplemented by very substantial aid from foundations such as did not exist a century ago, including the Ford Foundation and the Fund for the Advancement of Education as well as the Grant Foundation (acting thru the Educational Records Bureau of New York)—all of whom have recognized the transcendent importance of the problem i.t.a. has set itself to solve.

Chapter 6

Initial teaching orthographies
in general, and in particular

Thus far our discussion of methods of whatever type, and of phonemic media, has proceeded largely in terms of *reading*. Riemer, in a recently published book,[1] colloquially expressed but broadly researched and persuasive, has pointed out that the blighting effect of restricted vocabularies and long-deferred concern with word-building power not only affects the earliest grades but also carries forward into and thru high school and college and even graduate school as an inability to write simple, literate, intelligible English. He points out that there are a plethora of reading experts attached to our educational institutions, but few if any writing experts. There are an endless variety of reading curricula, but where are the writing curricula (writing as written expression, that is — not handwriting)? Researches on reading, especially beginning reading, are a dime a dozen, researches on primary grade composition, almost nonexistent. Writing has been treated, in the critically important early grades, largely as a mere byproduct, demanding and receiving only incidental attention.

There are *two* major factors in the conspicuous success which an i.t.m. such as i.t.a. achieves as compared with methods based on T.O. The first is the deferring of most of the difficulties with which T.O. methods must wrestle from the very beginning, until the time of the transition to T.O., when the child is sufficiently at home in the basic processes of reading and writing, more often than not fluently (in the

[1] George Riemer, *How they murdered the second "R"* (New York: W. W. Norton & Co., Inc., 1969).

simple, regular phonemic code), to take them in his stride. The second is that as soon as the phonemic code is fully mastered, usually in a period of a relatively few weeks, it opens up the child's entire comprehension, that is, hearing and speaking vocabulary, for reading and writing. It is this fact which accounts for the extraordinary increase in creative writing, impressively documented by Riemer,[2] which has been observed in nearly all i.t.a. classes.

There is an important corollary to this unrestricted reading and writing vocabulary which must not be overlooked in judging the results of some so-called experimental comparisons of i.t.a. with established T.O. methods, especially of the basal reading type: to employ for the experimental group an i.t.a. transliteration of the T.O. materials used for the control group is *not* impartiality but a half-portion comparison which examines only the relative simplicity and regularity of the two codes, suppressing arbitrarily the *consequences* of the superior simplicity of the i.t.a. code as expressed in the more rapid introduction of all the phonemes of English, opening up for reading and writing the child's entire hearing and speaking vocabulary, with the extraordinary increase in spontaneous creative writing already noted. Such a comparison is as heavily biased against i.t.a. as would be a comparison of the performance of a 1920 and a 1970 motor car, which insisted on employing for both the gasoline for which the 1920 car was designed.

This comment is not intended as a criticism of the first British experiment, which employed for the i.t.a. classes a transliteration of the widely used T.O. *Janet and John* series, for at that time there existed no teaching materials specifically designed for i.t.a., nor any objective experience as a basis for preparing such materials, with consequent delay. Incidentally, it offered an opportunity to test the simplicity factor by itself, apart from its important consequences, some of them not even fully envisaged at that time. Today, however, with several methods specifically designed for i.t.a., and more than a thousand items of i.t.a. materials already available, such biased and restricted comparisons are hardly excusable.

[2] *Ibid.*

Guide lines

Suggested criteria for a phonemic notation for English for general use, including a section on the influence of purpose on the decisions to be made in their application, are set forth in Appendix C, referred to in passing in Chapter 4. The evidence adduced in Chapter 5 should raise at least a strong presumption that use of a phonemic notation as an i.t.m. has an important contribution to make to beginning reading and writing. My purpose here is to examine the resources available for creating such a notation, the qualities to be sought, the pitfalls to be avoided, and the principles which should guide the final synthesis and application of such a code. If at times I may seem to write with more assurance than the immediately pertinent data warrant, I can only plead that 70 years of writing English phonemically (in shorthand) and nearly 50 years of active concern with the problems of spelling reform, including various items of research, have given me a more than ordinary basis for judgment.

The problem may be broken down into an examination of sounds and symbols and the principles which should govern the assignment of symbols to sounds, including the influence of the particular purpose to be achieved.

Sounds

In the choice of sounds to be distinguished, the twin dangers are sophistication and ambiguity. Talk of phonemes and their allophones, morphemes and allomorphs, is for the linguistic scholar, not the elementary school teacher or pupil. An initial teaching orthography should be the simplest in form and substance that will achieve its purpose. In particular, it should be phonemic rather then phonetic, making all those distinctions and only those distinctions which are semantically significant, and making only those distinctions readily recognizable by the average untrained ear. Incidentally, it should be broad enough to absorb the most important regional differences — a problem which will be discussed later.

Specifically, consider the 40 sounds distinguished by Pitman Shorthand, commonly classed as 24 consonants, 12 vowels, and 4 diphthongs, disregarding such sophistications as

whether the vowel sounds of *bait* or *boat* are in fact diphthongs, or whether the "vowel" sounds of *youth* and *few* are
different or the same, and if the same, whether they are both
consonant plus vowel or both true diphthongs. These 40
sounds are the only phonemic basis for writing English which
has been proved in practical experience by millions of writers
(of Pitmanic shorthand) for more than a century. If you will
subtract from the 44 characters of i.t.a. 4 characters: *c* (an
alternate for /k/); the reversed *z* (an alternate for /z/); the *wh*
ligature (a single character for the consonant cluster /hw/); and
the modified *r* (which merely signals that the preceding vowel
is to be pronounced as schwa); you will have remaining this
basic 40-sound structure. To these 40 phonemes must be
added some provision for schwa, which in shorthand writing
is usually disregarded or omitted, but which must be recognized and provided for by some means in longhand or print.
This phonemic basis is the soundest (no pun intended) for an
initial teaching orthography. Possible modifications to meet
particular purposes will be discussed later.

To maintain uniformity of symbolization in the face of regional differences in pronunciation, this basic code should
maintain distinctions which a large number of cultivated
speakers do make, even tho another large number of cultivated
speakers do not make them, e.g.:

1. Writing postvocalic /r/, which "r-keepers" pronounce,
but which "r-droppers" omit (as in *far*), or reduce to schwa
(as in *near*).

2. Writing *wh* (for /hw/), altho a substantial number of
speakers, especially southern British, do not distinguish it
from /w/.

3. Distinguishing the vowel of *father* and *calm* from the
vowel of *bother* and *comma,* as in most British pronunciation,
altho general American pronunciation does not make this
distinction. This has the added advantage that (except before
r and occasionally after *w*) it follows quite closely the T.O.
spellings with *a* and *o* respectively.

*Uniformity in symbolizing lesser divergencies will be greatly
facilitated by the tendency of each region to attach its own
values to the symbols.* For a textbook or dictionary key to
pronunciation, to be read rather than written, three ambiva-

lent symbols will further facilitate this, more particularly:

1. For the vowel of *ask, bath, aunt,* which varies regionally, but also unpredictably, between the vowels of *cam* and *calm,* with the former more usual in the United States.

2. For the vowel of *air, care, their,* which varies regionally between the vowels of *bat, bet,* or *bait;* use of the latter, as in Pitman Shorthand, causing the least confusion.

3. For the high front unstressed vowel, which Sir James Pitman has aptly named *schwi,* which combines most of the shortness of *i* in *bit* with much of the closeness of *ee* in *beet;* heard in the last vowel of *any,* the first vowel of *believe.*

Symbols

The symbols for a practicable initial teaching orthography may be derived from either of two sources, more fully discussed under "Phonemic notations and the Roman alphabet" in Chapter 4:

Standardizing the Roman alphabet, by assigning to each single letter, and to each digraph selected to represent those sounds for which the available single letters do not suffice, a single sound, keeping strictly within the resources of the universally available Roman alphabet (as exemplified by WES).

Supplementing the Roman alphabet, by assigning to each of the 23 useful letters (exclusive of *c, q,* and *x*) a single invariable value, and creating some 17 or more new symbols (as exemplified by i.t.a.).

A third theoretically possible source is *supplanting* the Roman alphabet, by creating, and making available on typewriters and composing machines thruout the world, some 41 wholly new characters, quite independent of the Roman alphabet; as specified by Shaw for his Proposed British Alphabet. This is an interesting philosophic speculation, but completely unrealistic in that it eliminates the indispensable factor of "self-reading" compatibility with T.O.

Assignment of symbols to sounds

An initial teaching orthography should have, so far as practicable, only one symbol for each sound, and should regard, so far as possible, the predominant T.O. spellings of sounds.

This aspect is important primarily for *writing*. Conversely, it should have, so far as practicable, only one sound for each symbol, and should regard, so far as possible, the predominant T.O. pronunciations of the symbols. This aspect is important primarily for *reading*.

Note that these two limitations are *not* just inverted state-ment of the same fact. Thus, the predominant *spellings* of the name-sounds of A, E, U are the letters *a, e, u*; but the predomi-nant *pronunciations* of the letters *a, e, u* are as in *bat, bet, but* respectively. Similarly, the commonest *spelling* of the pho-neme /z/ is the letter *s*, but the commonest *pronunciation* of the letter *s* is /s/. It is the ignoring of this second aspect which completely invalidates the data of W. R. Lee's 1957 study, *Spelling irregularity and reading difficulty in English.*[3]

In applying these criteria, a successful initial teaching or-thography must achieve a substantially "self-reading" degree of compatibility with T.O. – that is, a degree of similarity to the words and graphemes of T.O. such that the notation may be immediately readable by those familiar only with T.O., and that T.O. may be readable with little further study by those who have mastered the phonemic notation. It should achieve this goal, of course, with as few rules or exceptions, alterna-tive spellings, or ambiguous pronunciations as possible. Un-fortunately, however, once the basic 40-sounds, 40-symbols code has been determined, all further gains in compatibility must come from concessions from strictly phonemic symbol-ization, with a corresponding departure from complete sim-plicity. *This equation between simplicity and compatibility is the final, most searching test of the validity of a phonemic initial teaching orthography.*

It is in striking this balance between simplicity and compat-ibility that the chief differences between a spelling reform notation and an initial teaching orthography appear. A spelling reform notation, to be written as well as read by the general public, must emphasize maximum simplicity – that is, a mini-mum of rules or exceptions or alternatives, even at some ex-pense of compatibility. On the other hand, while almost any reasonably phonemic notation, regardless of idiosyncrasies of symbolization, may be learned far more easily than T.O., an initial teaching orthography stands or falls on the ease of

[3] London: University of London, Institute of Education, 1959.

transition to reading and writing T.O. Considerably greater emphasis on compatibility, thru alternate symbolizations, rules, or exceptions (*provided* that these affect a significant proportion of words), is therefore warranted; for these alternatives are, in effect, a preparatory phase of the transition, and mistakes due to wrong choice of alternatives during the temporary period of writing the initial teaching orthography are of no lasting importance.

To guide these crucial decisions, both in setting up and applying the code, objective data on the relative frequency, both of phonemes and graphemes, are greatly needed. So far as *writing*, more particularly learning to spell, is concerned, data on a dictionary basis (unweighted for the relative frequency of occurrence of particular words) may be sufficient, but for *reading*, which is the primary function of an initial teaching orthography, data which take into account frequency of occurrence on the printed page are considerably more significant. So far as phonemes and phoneme combinations are concerned, my *RF/Sounds,* first published in 1923, still provides the most significant data available — data which have been relied on in the creation of Zachrisson's Anglic,[4] and in the important revision of the British New Spelling in 1930, which Anglic influenced; in the construction of Ogden's Basic English, and of Pitman's i.t.a.; as well as a host of less well-known projects. For graphemes, Hanna's recent study[5] provides an exhaustive analysis of spellings of sounds in terms of *items* (number of different words) but none in terms of *occurrences* (relative frequency on a running words basis), the more important aspect for reading.[6] For an exhaustive analysis of graphemes, in terms both of occurrences and items, my recently published *RF/Spellings* provides at last authentic data, comparable in scope and accuracy to the phonemic data of *RF/Sounds.*

Pitfalls

Before turning to an examination of i.t.a. as the outstanding example of an initial teaching orthography of the *supplementing* type, and of WES as the most thoroly researched example

---

[4] Zachrisson, *Anglic.*

[5] Hanna *et al., Phoneme-grapheme correspondences.*

[6] See *RF/Spellings,* Ch. 1 and Appendixes A and B.

of the *standardizing* type, a word as to the commonest faults found in phonemic notations, whether devised as initial teaching orthographies or, more frequently, for spelling reform, without recognizing the more important differences in emphasis involved.

Phonemic faults common to both the supplementing and standardizing types include distinguishing too few, or occasionally too many, different phonemes; assigning existing single letters with too little regard for their predominant values in T.O.; and introducing too many rules or exceptions for phonemes or word groups of relatively infrequent occurrence.

Perhaps the most egregious fault, in any type of notation, is misuse of the letters *c*, *q*, and/or *x* for values wholly unrelated to their T.O. significations (e.g., for vowels or instead of consonant digraphs for wholly unrelated values such as *th*), for this involves the effort of dissociation from any previous familiarity, which is a constant offense against compatibility, and, for an initial teaching orthography, an eventual redissociation from the acquired alternative value. Closely related to this fault, in its psychologic impact, is the use of caps and/or small caps for values other than the corresponding lower-case letters.

Another somewhat less serious but nevertheless severe graphemic handicap is the attempt to base an entire new (but professedly Roman) alphabet on upper-case forms, which are inherently less legible for lack of ascenders and descenders, instead of on the lower-case forms which make up over 95% of our reading and at least 99% of all writing.

Yet another unnecessary handicap is the effort to provide a duplicate alphabet of upper-case as well as lower-case forms, and sometimes even two more alphabets of large and small cursive letters, instead of concentrating on a single lower-case form, to be written disjoined (manuscript writing) for handwriting, with an enlarged or heavier letter or a single diacritic (capsign) to identify capitals where desired.

The temptation to use diacritics is another pitfall which combines the disadvantages of both the supplementing and standardizing solutions, for a letter with a diacritic mark is, for the printer, just as much an additional character as a new design, and on the typewriter requires three strokes (letter, backspace, diacritic), unless the typewriter has been altered to provide a dead key, in which case it still requires two strokes.

For the standardizing, no-new-letter type of notation, to which I believe the immediate future of spelling reform chiefly belongs, because of the enormous difficulties of making new characters available in hundreds of type faces and sizes in tens of thousands of printing plants and on tens of millions of typewriters, the central problem is choice and assignment of digraphs. Here the commonest fault is failure to recognize that a digraph is a unit, quite independent of the values of the component letters, and should therefore be devised and assigned for maximum compatibility with T.O. usages, rather than striving for a forced or logical relationship to the component letters at the cost of a bizarre result.

i.t.a.

Analysis

i.t.a. is today beyond question the outstanding exemplar of a phonemic notation as an initial teaching medium. Table 8 presents the code in the form preferred by Sir James,[7] which is probably the most informative as well as the most "official" of several different arrangements currently in use by different publishers. Considering its antecedents, we find, quite predictably, that by our criteria its phonemic basis (that is, the number and nature of the sounds to be distinguished) rates practically 100%. The 40-sound foundation is supplemented by schwa, using both of the suggested devices: retaining any single letter of T.O., and a special symbol, the modified *r*, which is, in effect, a diacritic signaling that the immediately preceding vowel, stressed or unstressed, is to be pronounced as schwa.

Graphically, the code is greatly simplified, and its effectiveness correspondingly enhanced, by having only one form, corresponding to lower-case print, for each symbol; identifying capitals merely by a slight increase in size.

Assignment of the single letters of the basic code agrees

[7] Pitman and St. John, *Alphabets and reading*, p. 119.

Table 8   The Initial Teaching Alphabet

No.	Character	Name	Example	No.	Character	Name	Example
1.	æ	ain	æbl	23.	y	yay	yellœ
2.	b	bee	but	24.	z	zed or	zꙍ
3.	c	kee	cat			zee	
	d			25.	ꙅ	zess	aꙅ
4.	ḍ	did	ḍog	26.	wh	whee	whie
5.	ɛɛ	een	ɛɛḍh	27.	ḍh	chay	ḍhurḍh
6.	f	ef	fun	28.	ṭh	ith	ṭhin
7.	g	gay	gæt	29.	ᵵh	thee	ᵵhen
8.	h	hay	hay	30.	ʃh	ish	ʃhip
9.	ie	ide	ies	31.	ʒ	zhee	meʒue
10.	j	jay	jam	32.	ŋ	ing	siŋ
11.	k	kay	kiŋ	33.	ᴦ	er	herᴦ
12.	l	el	lip	34.	a	ahd	faᴦher
13.	m	em	man		a	ask	
14.	n	en	not	35.	a	at	at
15.	œ	ode	œpen	36.	au	aud	autum
16.	p	pee	pæ	37.	e	et	egg
	q			38.	i	it	it
17.	r	ray	rat	39.	o	og	on
18.	s	ess	sit	40.	u	ug	up
19.	t	tee	top	41.	ω	oot	bωk
20.	ue	une	ueꙅ	42.	ꙍ	ood	mꙍn
21.	v	vee	vois	43.	ou	oun	out
22.	w	way	wet	44.	oi	oin	oil
	x						

completely (except for the inclusion of *c* as well as *k*) with the long experience of the British New Spelling, as well as the spelling reform version of WES. In my judgment, for the purposes under consideration, these assignments cannot be improved upon.

Of the 20 new symbols supplied by i.t.a., 13 are easily recognizable ligatures of the digraphs employed by New Spelling and WES, which again are in complete agreement on 11 of these (all except the two symbols for *th*). Since these digraphs in turn are based largely on prevailing T.O. practice, their forms, altho more cumbersome in use than a simple unitary character, undoubtedly contribute somewhat to the ease of the all-important transition to T.O.

Most of the remaining 7 i.t.a. symbols (the majority being for phonemes of relatively low frequency) are obviously suggestive of familiar T.O. graphemes. The precise forms of some are perhaps debatable, but personally I regard criticisms of these details as altogether unprofitable at this time; for, assuming that some might be improved, the overall effect on teaching results would be too slight to be significantly measurable by any tests now available, and the encouragement which such tinkering would give to what Sir James has called "Babelization" would be unfortunate for all concerned. Personally, I doubt if a *significantly* better initial teaching orthography *of the supplementing type* can be devised. The one aspect that does abundantly warrant experimental determination is the choice between the *supplementing* type and the *standardizing,* no-new-letter type, of which more hereafter.

While certain aspects of the basic i.t.a. code itself, e.g., choice of relatively cumbersome symbol forms resembling familiar T.O. graphemes, instead of streamlined forms designed to save effort and space and therewith money (the aspect on which Shaw laid chief emphasis), tend to differentiate it from a spelling reform notation, the chief differences appear in the *application* of the code; the deliberate departures from strictly phonemic writing, thru rules and exceptions based on *T.O. practice* rather than *phonemic cues.* Collectively these enhance compatibility in ways which contribute directly to the all-important transition to reading and writing in T.O. This aspect has been too little understood or justly evaluated by some of the more vocal critics of i.t.a.

It is at this point that objective data are particularly valuable; nevertheless, subjective judgment finally enters in, in determining how small a gain in compatibility warrants an additional rule or exception. Thus, one of the most dependable phonic generalizations of T.O. is that where a single vowel is followed by a doubled consonant, the preceding vowel is short. In consequence, the i.t.a. rule retaining doubled consonants for a single sound where T.O. has doubled consonants, improves the compatibility of nearly 7,000 words in 100,000 running words, and preserves the exact T.O. forms of about 2,000. Similarly, some 70% of T.O. spellings of the /k/ phoneme involve the letter *c* to some extent; so that the i.t.a. practice of writing *c* (including *cc* and *ck*) where T.O. employs *c* for the /k/ sound, improves the compatibility of some 6,500 words out of 100,000, and retains the precise T.O. forms of some 1,200. Likewise, writing *y* where T.O. has *y* for the unstressed short vowel at the end of words like *pity,* improves the compatibility of some 4,000 words out of 100,000, and retains the precise T.O. forms of some 800. On the other hand, the rule or exception which writes *tch* after a vowel where T.O. has *tch,* but *ch* where it does not (writing *clutch* but *much, etch* but *eech, match* but *ranch,* etc.), which affects less than 1 word in 1,000 running words, is difficult to justify. In between lie such borderline cases as writing *nature* or *picture,* etc., as *naetuer* or *pictuer,* instead of *naecher* or *pic-cher,* altho current dictionaries no longer record the more formal pronunciation. These affect only about 2 words in 1,000, but offer a distinct advantage in preserving the root, which reappears in such derivatives as *native* or *pictorial.* On balance, it is unlikely that experimental tinkering with such minutiae would yield significant differences in overall results, as measured by any tests presently available.

To summarize, it would seem that for the present far more may be accomplished for education by research to explore and develop the full possibilities of this type of phonemic notation as an i.t.m., using the wealth of teaching materials already available in this particular medium, i.t.a., rather than by seeking for minor adjustments before the major factors have been fully explored.[8]

Progress to date

Rarely if ever has an educational innovation attracted so much attention or compiled so impressive a record in so short a period. To attempt to select and reproduce statistical evidence on particular points would be quite beyond the scope of this study. The most that can be done is to give a brief, largely quantitative overview of progress, and to refer the

[8] See, however, in Ch. 8, Sir James's own suggestions for future research.

reader to the more important published research findings, which should be consulted at first hand.

The first British experiment with i.t.a. was conducted by the Reading Research Unit established in 1960, jointly sponsored by the University of London Institute of Education and the National Foundation for Educational Research in England and Wales. This experiment included 873 children in the experimental group, beginning with 20 schools, with 33 schools providing control groups taught by T.O. In the fall of 1965 it was estimated that over 100,000 children in Great Britain were using i.t.a. The comprehensive survey by Warburton and Southgate, hereafter cited, which included questionnaires to all of the 163 local educational authorities in England and Wales, received 158 replies, indicating that 140 of the local education authorities were using i.t.a. to some extent. Of the total number of 16,868 infant schools (5 to 8 years) represented by those replying, 1,554 or 9.2% were using i.t.a. as of the summer of 1966, 5 years after the beginning of the initial experiment. Estimates by others, based on available data for the next three years, have indicated that by 1970 this figure would approximate 20%.

In the United States, where teaching with i.t.a. was begun in 1963, notably in Bethlehem, Pennsylvania, Cleveland, Ohio, and White Plains, New York, there has been no nation-wide survey comparable to that in Great Britain, but it is known that i.t.a. is being used to some degree in all 50 states and in at least 10% of all school districts.

Teaching materials for the first British experiment were limited to i.t.a. transliterations of the *Janet and John* series (both look-and-say and phonics methods) most widely used in Great Britain, together with an all-too-limited supply of reading books for the Book Corner, often provided by pasting i.t.a. text over the T.O. text. By 1966 i.t.a. materials were being provided by over 40 publishers in England and the United States, and by 1969 over 80 publishers and suppliers had produced over 1,200 items employing i.t.a.

Scarcely less remarkable than the rate of progress of i.t.a. in the schools has been the amount of research and experiment and discussion which has accompanied it. The primary factors for which experimental and control groups have been compared at appropriate intervals have been accuracy, speed, and comprehension. Unfortunately, but almost inevitably, these factors have usually been measured by tests devised for and validated by instruction in methods employing only T.O. Transliteration of such tests, when this was done for the earliest stages, by no means suffices to measure justly the superior capabilities usually resulting from i.t.a. instruction. (Development of more suitable tests is one of the items for future research discussed in Chapter 8.) Secondary factors usually investigated included the period and the manner in which the transition to T.O. occurred, and the effect of i.t.a. instruction on future ability to spell in T.O. Factors to which all too little attention has been given are the effect of i.t.a. on spontaneous and creative writing,[9] and its effect on the child himself.

The most adequate statistical reports on the British situation are those of Harrison (1964),[10] Downing (1964),[11] Downing *et al.* (1967),[12] and Warburton and Southgate (1969).[13] In the

[9] Riemer, *How they murdered the second "R."*

[10] Maurice Harrison, *Instant reading.* This includes, with much interesting historical background on the whole problem, interim reports on the Oldham participation in the first two years of the British experiment.

[11] John Downing, *The i.t.a. reading experiment* (London: Evans Brothers, Ltd., for the University of London Institute of Education, 1964). Three lectures delivered in 1963 and 1964, constituting in effect an interim report on the first two years of the three-year British experiment.

[12] John Downing *et al., The i.t.a. symposium: Research report on the British experiment with i.t.a.* (Slough, Buckinghamshire: National Foundation for Educational Research in England and Wales, 1967). Interpretation of this official report, with its evaluations or commentaries by 13 educators, should be qualified by the comments of Sir James Pitman in *Alphabets and reading,* Ch. 9.

[13] F. W. Warburton and Vera Southgate, *i.t.a.: An independent evaluation* (London: John Murray and W. & R. Chambers, 1969). This is an extensive survey of i.t.a. in England and Wales, sponsored by the British Schools Council, covering the first five years (1961–1966). Its conclusions are summarized under three heads: Conclusions drawn from the verbal evidence; from the research evidence; from the total evidence. Overall, the conclusions, altho cautious, are impressively favorable. The one somewhat negative conclusion, "The advantages of i.t.a. do not last" beyond the transition, seized on by opponents of i.t.a., is, in my own judgment, chiefly if not wholly accounted for by the fact that curricula in general are necessarily adjusted to the great majority of pupils who are still being taught by T.O., thus enforcing on the i.t.a. pupils a period of more or less marking time to get back into step.

United States the six issues of *the i.t.a. foundaeshon report* [14] published in 1966 and 1967 include a bibliography of over 400 authored articles (including some British items) and over 50 unauthored articles (which latter number would be increased by hundreds if "letters to the editor" were included), together with 44 research abstracts. In addition, Pitman gives an instructive summary, by Tanyzer and Block, of i.t.a. research in the United States,[15] pointing out significant differences between the British and American programs. He also gives a selected bibliography [16] of some 160 items, American as well as English.

In summary, without prejudice to the as yet undemonstrated possibilities of WES as an i.t.m., discussed in the next section, the preponderance of the evidence would seem to justify Sir James Pitman's challenge, "Why wait any longer?" [17]

WES

World English Spelling (WES) is, beyond question, the most thoroly researched no-new-letter phonemic notation for English before the public today. The basic spelling reform version shown in Chapter 4, Table 5, has been evolved thru investigation and discussion by the ablest specialists on both sides of the Atlantic over a period of 60 years. The i.t.m. version shown here in Table 9 differs chiefly in adding *c* and in incorporating in its application the major departures from phonemic writing in favor of T.O. practice more fully described under i.t.a.

Since both WES and i.t.a. derive most of their phonemic structure and much of their symbolization from the same sources, it is not surprising that they are virtually identical *except* for the elimination of new characters by use of digraphs instead of ligatures or new letter forms. More particularly, the phonemic basis of 40 phonemes is identical, but WES treats schwa by simple rules only, without a special diacritic symbol.

[14] Hempstead, N.Y.: The Initial Teaching Alphabet Foundation at Hofstra University, 1966, 1967.
[15] Pitman and St. John, *Alphabets and reading*, Appendix III.
[16] *Ibid.*, pp. 331–338.
[17] *Ibid.*, Ch. 14.

Table 9 WES as an initial teaching medium

Consonants
    As in

Vowels and diphthongs
    As in

p	*p*ay, ha*pp*y, ca*p*	**a**	*a*t, m*a*n; *a*sk; *a*bout, dat*a*
b	*b*ay, ru*bb*er, ca*b*	**aa**	*a*lms, f*a*ther, b*ah*; (*a*sk)
t	*t*own, le*t*ter, bi*t*	**ar**	*ar*my, m*ar*ket, f*ar*
d	*d*own, la*dd*er, bi*d*	**e**	*e*dge, m*e*n, s*ai*d, h*ea*d, a*ny*
c	*c*ame, a*cc*ount, publi*c*; ba*c*k	**ae**	*a*g*e*, m*ai*n, s*ay*, gr*ea*t
k	*k*eep, wee*k*; ba*ck*; expe*c*t; *q*uite	**aer**	*air*, c*are*, th*eir*
g	*g*ame, ra*gg*ed, ba*g*; e*x*act	**i**	*i*t, h*i*m, prett*y*, g*i*ve
f	*f*ast, o*ff*ice, *ph*otogra*ph*, sa*f*e	**ee**	*ea*ch, h*e*re, s*ee*, b*e*
v	*v*ast, ne*v*er, sa*v*e	**o**	*o*n, b*o*ther, n*o*t; w*a*s, wh*a*t
thh	*th*ought, no*th*ing, bo*th*	**au**	*au*thor, l*aw*, *a*ll, w*a*ter, *ough*t
th	*th*at, ra*th*er, wi*th*	**or**	*or*der, n*or*th, f*or*; st*or*y, m*ore*
s	*s*eal, le*ss*on, *c*ity, ra*c*e, ba*s*e	**u**	*u*p, *o*ther, b*u*t, s*o*me, t*ou*ch
z	*z*eal, pu*zz*le, i*s*, rai*s*e, si*z*e	**oe**	*o*ld, n*o*te, g*oe*s, s*o*, c*oa*l, sh*ow*
sh	*sh*all, pre*ss*ure, na*ti*on, wi*sh*	**uu**	f*u*ll, s*u*re, sh*ou*ld, g*oo*d
zh	*j*abot, plea*s*ure, vi*si*on, rou*ge*	**oo**	f*oo*l, m*o*ve, gr*ou*p, r*u*le, t*oo*
ch	*ch*eck, *ch*ur*ch*, wat*ch*	**ie**	*i*ce, t*ie*, k*i*nd, m*igh*t, b*y*
j	*j*ust, *g*eneral, sta*ge*, *j*u*dge*	**ou**	*ou*t, p*ou*nd, n*ow*, b*ough*
m	*m*ight, com*m*on, the*m*	**oi**	*oi*l, p*oi*nt, b*oy*
n	*n*ight, din*n*er, the*n*	**ue**	*u*se, m*u*sic, d*ue*, f*ew*
ng	thi*ng*, lo*ng*, goi*ng*, si*ng*le	**er**	furth*er*, coll*ar*, mot*or*, murm*ur*
nk	thi*nk*, ba*nk*, u*nk*le, a*nk*le	**ur**	f*ur*ther, h*er*, *ear*ly, f*ir*st, w*or*k
l	*l*ate, fe*ll*ow, dea*l*		
r	*r*ate, ma*rr*ied, dea*r*		
w	*w*et, for*w*ard, *o*ne, q*u*ick		
wh	*wh*ich, every*wh*ere		
y	*y*et, be*y*ond, milli*on*; an*y*; *y*ou	For teaching purposes, use	
h	*h*ad, be*h*ind, *w*ho	only lower-case letter forms.	

Separate by a dot successive letters which might otherwise be read as a digraph —

short.hand, mis.hap, en.gaej, man.kiend
gae.ety, ree.elect, hie.est, loe.er, influu.ens, pou.er, emploi.ee

The assignments of the 24 single letters employed (excluding *q* and *x* in both notations) is identical, and 12 of the 13 ligatured symbols of i.t.a. transliterate directly into the corresponding digraphs of WES. Of the 7 remaining i.t.a. symbols, WES eliminates the alternate forms for *z* and *r*, and for the rest substitutes the digraphs *zh, ng, aa, oo, uu,* of which only *zh* and *uu* are wholly strange.

In applying the basic code, the spelling rules and exceptions of i.t.m. WES are, for the sake of greater compatibility with T.O., virtually identical with i.t.a., except for eliminating a few marginal details of insignificant effect, such as the *tch* alternative previously referred to, or the writing of *judge* as *judzh* instead of *juj*. This agreement has been maintained partly for the reasons adduced by i.t.a. but also to facilitate experimental comparisons between WES and i.t.a. without introducing additional independent variables other than the fundamental difference between the supplementing and standardizing types. WES thus becomes, in effect, a Roman alphabet paraphrase of i.t.a., keeping strictly within the resources of the universally available Roman alphabet.

The case for employing new characters not in the universally available Roman alphabet rests on the logical premise that a simple phonemic notation should have an explicit unitary character (a standardized digraph is an explicit *symbol*) for each phoneme, and on the assumption that a beginning student, especially an infant, will be confused by the fact that the value of a digraph is rarely if ever a fusion of the values of the separate letters — e.g., the sound of *th* in *then* is not that of *t* plus *h* in *shorthand;* *ng* in *spring* is not the *n* plus *g* in *engage;* the sound of *au* in *author* is not a fusion of the vowel sounds of *bat* and *but;* *ie* in *tie* is not a fusion of the vowel sounds of *bit* and *bet;* etc., etc. To this assumption there are at least three replies.

1. The number of digraphs, exclusive of doubled consonants, in the leading languages of Western Europe ranges from 5 or 6 for Spanish or Italian to 22 for Dutch, with a median of 12 or 14 for French or German, yet, so far as I am aware, no spelling reform movement in any of these countries has included proposals to create new single characters to replace these digraphs.

2. Misleading juxtapositions, such as in *shorthand* or *engage,* are so infrequent as to be almost negligible, and in any case may be separated by a dot (e.g., *short.hand, en.gage*) in the earliest stages of learning, if that be deemed necessary.

3. So far as either the theoretic or practical objections are

concerned, a ligature *below* a digraph, used if desired at its first introduction or during the first weeks of learning, makes it just as much a unitary symbol as the ligature above or between the component parts of the majority of the i.t.a. ligatured symbols — e.g., i.t.a. ᴕu, ᵻe; WES ọu, ịe.

If it can be demonstrated that the educational results attainable with WES are at least comparable with those attained by i.t.a., certain important advantages follow, both in the classroom and thereafter.

In the classroom, for the pupil it obviates learning to read, and especially to write, 20 new characters which will shortly be abandoned. For the teacher it facilitates preparation, on any standard typewriter, of supplementary teaching materials adapted to particular situations. For both pupil and teacher it permits use of the standard keyboard typewriter as a teaching instrument in the earliest grades, the great possibilities of which were demonstrated by Wood and Freeman [18] more than 35 years ago.

For the adult abroad who has been taught English as a second language with the help of an i.t.m., WES offers the exciting possibility of continuing to use it as an auxiliary medium of international communication; *reading* T.O. but *writing* in WES, thereby bypassing the considerable added burden of learning to write, i.e., to spell T.O. Incidentally, for the native adult who gets fed up with some of the grosser idiosyncrasies of T.O., it interposes no obstacle to carrying over into his own personal writing such phonemic forms as the spirit moves him to retain.

Experimental comparisons

Such possibilities as the above, both in and out of the classroom, give point and even urgency to controlled experimentation comparing WES with i.t.a. In due course there should be a thoro study of the comparative discriminability of ligatured characters such as those of i.t.a. and simple digraphs such as those in WES, whether in isolation (the least signifi-

---

[18] Ben D. Wood and Frank N. Freeman, *An experimental study of the educational influences of the typewriter in the elementary school classroom* (New York: The Macmillan Company, 1932).

cant), or embedded in words, or in context, but the foregoing reasons abundantly justify immediate experimental comparisons between the present forms of i.t.a. and i.t.m. WES.

Since abundant teaching materials of high quality, from many publishers, are already available for i.t.a., and since methods employing a phonemic i.t.m. will be essentially the same for either notation, the simplest as well as most unbiased source of teaching materials for WES will be transliteration into WES, for the experimental group, of the particular i.t.a. materials selected for the control group; permission for which, for legitimate experimental purposes, should be readily obtainable, not only from the Initial Teaching Alphabet Foundation but also from most publishers.

Transliteration *from i.t.a.* to WES is a relatively simple matter, calling for little more than familiarity with WES and the single-page transliteration chart shown in Table 10. Transliteration *from T.O.* to WES, to provide supplementary materials *in a form consistent with i.t.a.*, is a more involved affair, for which the 4-page transliteration guide in Appendix E will be found helpful. A detailed analysis of WES spellings, independent of maximum correlation with i.t.a., will be found in the "Guide lines" section of the *WES Dictionary*.[19] Suggestions in connection with experimental objectives or procedures will be presented in Chapter 8.

[19] Godfrey Dewey, *World English Spelling* (WES) *dictionary* (Lake Placid Club, N.Y.: Simpler Spelling Association, 1969).

Table 10   Transliteration chart from Pitman's Initial Teaching Alphabet to World English Spelling

i.t.a.	WES	i.t.a. key word	i.t.a.	WES	i.t.a. key word
p	p	pen	ᴡh	wh	when
b	b	bed	y	y	yes
t	t	tree	h	h	hat
d	d	dog	a	a	cap
c	c	cat	ɑ	aa	father
k	k	key	(2) (ɑr)	ar	(army)
g	g	leg	e	e	egg
f	f	feet	æ	ae	face
v	v	voice	(2) (ær)	aer	(air)
þh	thh	three	i	i	milk
ꝥh	th	the	ee	ee	key
s	s	spoon	o	o	box
z	z	zebra	au	au	ball
(1) ʒ	(z)	daisy	(2) (or)	or	(order)
ꝕh	ch	chair	u	u	up
j	j	jug	œ	oe	over
m	m	man	ω	uu	book
n	n	nest	ꙍ	oo	spoon
ŋ	ng	ring	ie	ie	fly
(2) (ŋk)	nk	(ink)	σu	ou	out
l	l	letter	σi	oi	oil
(3) r	r	red	ue	ue	use
ɼ *	(r)	girl	(3) *	er	(over)
w	w	window	(3) *	ur	(first)

(1) For i.t.a. ʒ, WES writes *z* in all cases.

(2) i.t.a. writes WES *nk, ar, aer, or* as shown, but does not distinguish these as separate symbols.

(3) For i.t.a. ɼ, which merely signals that the preceding vowel, whether unstressed or stressed, is to be pronounced as schwa, WES writes *r* in all cases.

　　For unstressed schwa, WES usually writes *e* (*er*); unless unstressed *a, i,* or *o* (or *u not* followed by *r*) occurs in T.O.

　　For stressed schwa, which occurs only before *r*, WES writes *u* (*ur*) in all cases.

Chapter 7

World English and initial teaching media

The potentially enormous values of a single internationally accepted auxiliary language, to be taught in every nation as a second language, along with the mother tongue, for purposes of world-wide international communication, are today beyond question. The debatable question is: what language will best realize these possibilities?

Achievement of the potential values of such an international auxiliary language (IAL) depends on *two* factors: the intrinsic merits of the language chosen and the degree of use which can be achieved. And the degree of use, in turn, depends on two factors: the intrinsic ease of learning the language chosen and the degree of motivation or other influences to assure that it will be learned.

In the matter of grammar and syntax, including regularity of inflections and logical derivation of different parts of speech from a single root, a good *a priori* case can be made for an artificial as against a natural language. When it comes to vocabulary, however, those constructed languages which attempt to be eclectic instead of completely arbitrary prove to be on examination little more than a somewhat biased selection from the Indo-European group, which is far from being a helpfully world-wide eclecticism—while those languages which are completely arbitrary impose a heavy and repellent burden on *all* potential users indiscriminately. On the other hand, English, with its cosmopolitan vocabulary and grammatical simplicity, as well as natural gender and normal sentence structure, offers these particular advantages of an artificially constructed language to a considerable degree, along with the immense additional appeal of a living language

75

and literature, already more widely diffused than any other.

More than a century ago, Jakob Grimm, sometimes referred to as the father of comparative philology, wrote regarding the international language problem:

> English may be considered the language of the world out of Europe, and this idiom . . . has attained an incomparable degree of fluency, and appears destined by nature more than any other that exists to become the world's language. Did not a whimsical, antiquated orthography stand in the way, the universality of this language would be still more evident, and we other Europeans may esteem ourselves fortunate that the English nation has not made this discovery.[1]

Even under that heavy handicap, English has made, in the intervening century, enormous progress toward becoming the dominant international language. Pitman [2] estimates that, in addition to 255 million whose mother tongue is English, at least 250 million more learn English as an auxiliary, and speculates that the total may reach 600 million. The old cry of linguistic imperialism, raised by those who would prefer an artificial IAL, rings hollow today when it is realized that the newly created nations all over the world are clamoring insistently for aid in the study and teaching of English, even in formerly colonial areas where some other European language has been predominant, and that Russia not only is not obstructing such efforts but also is itself teaching, in its own schools, more English than any other second language.[3]

As for the forces which would influence general adoption of World English as compared with even the best of artificial languages, the comparative progress of World English would be like taking a power boat down a swiftly flowing river as

---

[1] Vaile, *Our accursed spelling*, p. 65.

[2] Pitman and St. John, *Alphabets and reading*, p. 263.

[3] "Meeting the challenge of English teaching abroad" (A report of the deliberations and recommendations of a conference of English language education specialists convened by the Center for Applied Linguistics at the request of the International Cooperation Administration, Washington: Center for Applied Linguistics of the Modern Language Association of America, May 1961), pp. 1–2.

compared with paddling a canoe upstream. The artificial language is at best a utilitarian mechanism, cold and dead, like a punch card, whereas a phonemic i.t.m. such as i.t.a. or WES, mastery of which carries with it a serviceable *reading* knowledge of T.O., admits immediately to the wonderfully rich resources of English literature and the already world-wide diffusion of the English language press and radio and TV. World travel and world trade, as well as world culture, are constantly enlarging the areas in which English is, even now, in effect the accepted IAL; for example, English is already the official language of international aviation. To move with these forces, rather than against them, is the surest, swiftest way to the desired goal.

Speech i.t.a.

For the teaching of English as a second language, whether at home (in an English-speaking country) or abroad (in a non-English-speaking country), the T.O. roadblock operates with peculiar force. In either milieu, it must be assumed that most of the words in the vocabulary which the learner is acquiring will be encountered first in print rather than in speech, so that the written representation must be relied on more completely to convey the phonemic pattern, instead of merely forming an association with an oral pattern already familiar; while in a non-English-speaking environment the learner is further deprived of the guidance of hearing constantly, outside the classroom, many of the spoken words which he must associate with their written counterparts. For this reason, a phonemic notation as an i.t.m. is of even greater value than for the native English-speaking learner, whether child or adult. Pitman has pointed out the importance of conveying this additional information, more particularly:

"A. Information about the degree of stress, or lack of it, on the vowel in certain words and syllables.

"B. Information about the accompanying changes in vowel sounds that occur in unstressed syllables and words (which in other sentences may be stressed)." [4]

[4] Pitman and St. John, *Alphabets and reading*, pp. 266–267.

To meet this problem, Sir James has devised for i.t.a. an extremely ingenious notation, shown in Table 11, for supplying this information "without changing any of the i.t.a. characters and spellings and without reducing the compatibility between the learning medium and what is eventually to be mastered." [5] In his own words, slightly abridged:

The differences between World i.t.a.[6] and domestic i.t.a. can be summarized as follows:

(1) Whenever a syllable or word is to receive a primary stress, it is printed in semi-bold type but in the normal size (Table 11, all lines).

(2) Whenever the vowel in a syllable or word is to become unstressed (the relaxed vowel or *schwa*) . . . and is to be spoken in its weak form, it is printed in smaller type and aligned with the base of the main type line (Table 11, all lines).

(3) Whenever the vowel in a syllable or word is to be changed to the unstressed *i* (which it is convenient to call *schwi*), it is likewise printed in smaller type but it aligns with the top of the main type line (Table 11, last 4 lines).

Happily, the same technique may be applied in the same manner to the no-new-letter phonemic notation of WES.

Research on the practical application of this technique is already in progress in Western Nigeria under the auspices of the University of Ibadan, and as a result books and other teaching materials printed in Speech i.t.a. are now available for teachers of English in other areas. It is to be hoped that further experimental evidence will be accumulated in the near future.

In the same chapter just cited,[7] Pitman has pointed out a further advantage of i.t.a. as a corrective or at least a damper on the "Babelization" which tends to develop regionally, both at home and abroad, for lack of any clearly discernible or dependable relation between the written and the spoken

---

[5] *Ibid.*, pp. 266–268.

[6] More recently referred to as "Speech i.t.a."

[7] Pitman and St. John, *Alphabets and reading*, pp. 271–274.

Table 11 Speech i.t.a. exemplified

it is not for yoo. yoo aulredy hav wun and too hav

given mee nun wood hav been unfær. for, yoo

must admit, yoo wood œnly hav wæsted it. wood

yoo hav kept it and clœsd the dor too in mie

fæs? and, for yet anuther reeson it wos after

aull mie turn and, if it wos not, yoo never

sed sœ.

at the ekwætor the dæ is twelv ours loŋ. every

dæ from sundæ too saturdæ.　the printed pæj is

reformd in œnly sum respects in this æj ov the

wurld's dœtæj.

79

word. The point is well taken, and again it may be noted that it applies equally to WES.

In summary, it may fairly be said that the advantages of a phonemic notation as an i.t.m., described under that heading in Chapter 6, apply with even greater force in the teaching of English as a second language, thereby contributing significantly to the second of the three major objectives of spelling reform cited in Chapter 4.

Chapter 8

Future research

It must not be supposed from the emphasis placed on our present English spelling as the principal roadblock to reading, and on a phonemic initial teaching medium as, for the present, the most effective detour past that roadblock, that that technique is fully developed or is being offered as a panacea for all the problems of learning to read. Indeed, even if or when the roadblock itself is finally dismantled by the ultimate solution, a phonemic spelling reform, the underlying problems of the learning process, applicable to any subject matter, will, of course, remain. The impact on education, however, of the evidence thus far developed by i.t.a., is already so great that I must agree fully with Sir James that "it would seem that eventually many if not all researches into the teaching of reading which have hitherto been conducted with the orthodox alphabet(s) and spelling as the medium will need to be redone or at any rate revalidated." [1] This chapter will discuss briefly projected research under three heads: i.t.a., WES, and in general.

i.t.a.[2]

Possible new lines of investigation include:

*1. The selection of the vocabulary used in i.t.a. primers, teaching apparatus, and supporting reading books needs to

---

[1] Pitman and St. John, *Alphabets and reading*, p. 247.

[2] *Ibid.* This section is abridged, so far as possible in Sir James's own words, from Ch. 13, "Future i.t.a. research." Items marked * are the same for WES; items marked † are essentially similar.

be reviewed if the fullest benefit is to be gained from the new medium.

*2. Experience will also enable us to judge more precisely what is the optimum moment for the transition to orthodox print.

*3. An investigation will, I hope, be carried out into the effect of using i.t.a. even with children in secondary schools who have not managed to gain a full measure of fluency when reading orthodox print.

*4. It has so far been widely accepted that children are not ready to start learning to read until they have a mental age of six and a half. . . . This may be true when children are faced at the outset with words spelt in the orthodox manner, but with i.t.a. it would seem that a lower mental age is sufficient for a start to be made – provided, as has been argued earlier, that pupils possess an adequate level of linguistic ability.

*5. If the average child learns to read somewhere around one or two years earlier, it will necessitate a reconsideration of the remainder of the curriculum during the subsequent school years. It may well alter accepted views on children's rates of development and on the levels of attainment to be expected at various ages. Eventually it will be necessary to devise new tests of reading accuracy, speed, and comprehension because the existing tests are based on standards expected of children taught with all the frustrations of orthodox spelling.

†6. The employment of electric or very simply operated manual typewriters to help very young children to read and write, employed by Professor O. K. Moore of Yale University,[3] also lends support to the view that the accepted criterion for reading readiness is mistaken. Moore has shown that electric typewriters built for the purpose can be used by a 2- to 3-year-old child who is not yet able to manipulate a pencil effectively.

7. It is possible that color could be effective in reinforcing even further the relationship between shape and sound provided by i.t.a. When color is applied to the orthodox alphabet(s) and spelling there must inevitably be a residual conflict between shape and color, but with i.t.a. – thanks to its con-

---

[3] The "typewriters" employed by Moore were in fact elaborate and costly teaching machines. For use of a standard typewriter, see Wood and Freeman, *An experimental study*, cited in Ch. 6.

sistency and invariability—color and shape can always be in harmony.

*8. Thruout this book it has been stressed that i.t.a. is a teaching medium only, and that it does not necessitate any change of teaching method; that it can bring better results both with look-and-say and phonic methods, or with a mixture of the two. . . . There are however already indications that minor adjustments to the mixture of existing methods may be advisable if the benefits of i.t.a. are to be exploited to the full.

9. The Initial Teaching Alphabet can be adapted for use with other languages besides English.

†10. . . . Now that i.t.a. has been proved to be effective and it is already being used widely I believe there is a very strong case for caution before tampering with it. I do not wish to follow the example of my grandfather who was rightly criticized for never leaving Fonotypy alone. . . . I think it would be wise to enforce a moratorium on changes in the i.t.a. characters and spellings during the next twenty years or so—until, say, 1990. For the moment the benefits likely to come from any future changes or additions to i.t.a. or in the principles by which it represents words (e.g., the extent to which it falls short of absolute phonetic truth) are likely to be more than offset by the dislocation and confusion any change would cause among teachers and by the outdating of the hundreds of i.t.a. books already in print.[4]

WES

Inasmuch as WES has yet to prove its ability, as an i.t.m., to produce results comparable with those already impressively demonstrated by i.t.a., its research problems are broader and more immediate.

The first and most basic studies should be controlled experimentation, preferably extending over the first three years, comparing experimental (WES) groups with control (i.t.a.) groups, to test the hypothesis: WES will attain results in reading and writing comparable with the results now being achieved with i.t.a.

[4] Compare Ch. 6, p. 65.

For the first experiments:

1. Pupils should represent a fairly wide spectrum of average children, matched as closely, in all significant variables, as circumstances permit.

2. Teachers for the experimental groups should preferably be those who have had previous favorable experience with i.t.a. but are open-minded as to the possibilities of WES, *or* the same teachers who teach the control groups.

3. Teaching materials for WES should be, as suggested in Chapter 6, substantially transliterations into WES of the leading series used for the control groups — e.g., the *Early-to-read* series of Initial Teaching Alphabet Publications, Inc., or the *Reading program* of the Educational Research Council of America. For a pilot experiment, WES text could be pasted over the i.t.a. text. Workbooks would require slight adjustments for unavoidable discrepancies such as elimination of the reversed *z* and modified *r* of i.t.a.; with slight revision of teachers manuals, largely for the same reasons.

The first variation to be explored, using subgroups, should be the possible use of a ligature below the WES digraphs: whether (a) briefly, on the blackboard, in introducing each symbol; or (b) briefly, by pupils, following the first introduction of each symbol; or (c) briefly (for two or three weeks) in the textbooks, at the first introduction of each symbol.

The second variation to be explored, by a subgroup or groups, should be use of ordinary typewriters by the pupils, in line with the findings of Wood and Freeman.[5]

For the first experiments, it will undoubtedly be necessary to use, *for both groups,* for measurement of the basic factors of accuracy, speed, and comprehension in reading, as well as related factors concerned with writing and spelling, tests based wholly on experience with T.O. methods; transliterated, of course, into WES and i.t.a. when administered to pupils who have not yet made the transition to T.O., but nevertheless structured and rated on the basis of the limitations imposed by T.O. Pitman has pointed out[6] the unsuitability of existing tests "based on standards expected of children taught with all the frustrations of orthodox spelling" to measure

---

[5] Wood and Freeman, *An experimental study,* p. 184.
[6] In his fifth suggestion for future i.t.a. research, cited on p. 82.

justly the relatively higher achievements to be expected with i.t.a. This factor, of course, tends to cancel out in comparing two phonemic media such as WES and i.t.a. Inevitably, however, the results of such experiments, whether for WES or i.t.a., will be compared with the results attained with T.O. methods. Accordingly I regard the development of tests, structured and rated on the basis of results demonstrated or to be anticipated with phonemic initial teaching media, as being high on the list of future research projects.

Be it noted also at this point that 6 of Pitman's 10 suggestions for i.t.a. research (those marked with *) apply equally for WES, and that 2 more (those marked with †) are essentially similar for WES.

In general

As further evidence that supporters of phonemic initial teaching media are not complacent regarding the contribution, important tho it is, that such media can make to the overall problems of written communication, plans for an interdisciplinary, post-doctoral Reading-Writing Research Institute, to be established preferably at a leading university, to investigate in depth many or most of the processes involved in reading and writing, have been under consideration by distinguished scholars since 1967. Conferences sponsored by the Simpler Spelling Association, and made possible by a planning fund from the Grant Foundation, have been held to formulate specific proposals. An outline of the present formulation by these conferences follows.

The Reading-Writing Research Institute will serve two major purposes:

1. To update reading instruction for different types of communities, basing methods and materials on available research in orthography, linguistics, psychology, sociology, education, and related disciplines.

2. To conduct and promote research on reading processes thru studies of (a) pupil learning, and (b) teacher education.

Orthography—the representation of speech sounds by letters, punctuation, and blank spaces—is a major concern in the teaching of reading and writing, and in information theory it is basic to the science and technology of electronically encoding and decoding language. The studies by Dewey dealing with the relative frequency of occurrence of the simple sounds and commoner sound combinations of English, and with the relative frequency of occurrence of the spellings of sounds and the pronunciations of spellings in the same material investigated, provide one important basis for scientific studies of encoding (writing) and decoding (reading).

Altho a spate of studies have been reported on reading, very little scientific information is available on the *nature of the reading process.* Hence, one goal for the Reading-Writing Research Institute is a multidisciplinary approach to the study of the perceptual and cognitive processing of graphic signals at the phoneme-grapheme and higher levels of linguistic structure.

In terms of educational objectives, the Reading-Writing Research Institute proposes two approaches to the experimental study of the reading process as a means of improving instruction in reading and writing:

1. Pupil learning — preparation for different types of beginning reading programs, category-cue-probability learning required for word perception in materials printed in traditional orthography or selected initial teaching alphabets, and other relevant studies.

2. Teacher education — effect on pupil achievement in the classroom when the teacher (by means of demonstration-laboratory courses) attains measurable, functional skills and/or knowledge in phonemics-orthography-symbol perception, motivation for verbal learning, differential psychology as a basis for differentiated instruction, concept formation and thinking (comprehension), and other relevant learning.

The total program of research in the Reading-Writing Research Institute has implications and applications in five areas of human endeavor:

1. Cultural — e.g., what can be done to facilitate the learning of children and adults after differences in dialects, syntax, etc., have been identified in various subcultures?

2. Pedagogic — e.g., how will research on reading and writing (including spelling) be translated into scientifically based initial teaching media, methods, and materials of instruction?

3. Psychologic — e.g., how can better understandings of perceptual and cognitive functions in reading be used to take advantage of the motivations of different cultural groups at different age levels, and to devise appropriate methods for developing perceptual skills and cognitive abilities?

4. Economic — e.g., how will the research (a) produce reduced costs of printing and other forms of graphic communication, (b) improve learning rates in reading and writing, (c) reduce school failures and dropouts, (d) facilitate "computer" reading of typed or printed material, etc.?

5. Political — e.g., what applications will the research findings have for improving communication between political units within the United States and internationally?

Such a research program can make extremely important contributions toward mastery of the process which lies at the root of all education, from kindergarten to college — reading and writing.

Epilog

We have seen that for more than a century English spelling has been recognized as the chief obstacle to the spread of English as the predominant international second language of the world, but that nevertheless, so strong has been the pressure of other factors, it has already made substantial progress toward that goal.

We have seen, too, that for at least two centuries a host of concerned individuals and a number of organizations, on both sides of the Atlantic, commanding from time to time an impressive array of philologists, lexicographers, other linguistic scholars, and occasionally men of affairs, have sought by various means to influence directly the spelling habits of their own adult generation, mostly with negligible or at best ephemeral results. We have examined also the traditional arguments commonly put forward by opponents of spelling reform, as well as the real obstacles which, in my judgment, continue to preclude any likelihood of influencing significantly the reading and writing habits of the present adult generation.

We have seen further that for at least four centuries English spelling has been regarded as the chief roadblock to learning to read and write, and that for more than a century a number of serious efforts have been made, both in this country and in Great Britain, to detour this roadblock by employing various forms of transitional reading media which taught the pupil to read and write with a considerable degree of fluency in a rational, relatively phonemic medium before facing up to the rigors of traditional orthography. We have sought to determine also why, in the face of uniformly impressive results, none of these previous methods survived and took root, and have examined some of the favorable factors, not heretofore present, which have influenced thus far the impressive progress of Pitman's i.t.a. and would in large measure affect similarly its Roman alphabet paraphrase—WES as an i.t.m.

Where do we go from here?

As a matter of tactics, Sir James is fully justified in expressly disavowing any spelling reform purpose for i.t.a., for a war on two fronts — the teaching of reading and advocacy of adult spelling reform — would greatly increase the likelihood of defeat on both. Also, it is quite true that some of the strongest and most distinctive features of i.t.a., the sacrifices of strict phonemic accuracy to a greater degree of compatibility with T.O., would be liabilities rather than assets in a spelling reform notation. As a matter of strategy, however, it is inevitable that use of phonemic initial teaching media such as i.t.a. or WES as the predominant approach to learning to read and write T.O., regardless of any other declared or undeclared purpose, merely because they prove to be the most efficient and effective means of instruction, will, within two or three decades, produce an adult generation for whom most of the real obstacles to spelling reform, cited in Chapter 4, will no longer exist — a generation conditioned not only to accept or welcome but even to demand a spelling reform which will eliminate for the future the dual approach to a single problem. In other words, the T.O. fortress, which for centuries has successfully withstood all frontal assaults, may be outflanked by an educational reform which pays its way handsomely as it goes, ignoring the fortress, and arrives in due course at the desired goal.

For those interested chiefly in the teaching of reading and writing, the lesson is clear: to encourage and adopt phonemic initial teaching media, more particularly i.t.a. and/or WES, and develop their full possibilities by research such as here suggested. For those concerned primarily with reaching the ultimate solution, a phonemic spelling reform for general use, which will render a separate and distinct initial teaching medium unnecessary, the watchword is patience, not forcing the issue prematurely. Perhaps by the close of the present millennium, we who have been wandering for 400 (not 40) years in the T.O. wilderness may find ourselves in sight of the promised land.

Appendixes

Delimitation of spellings in Appendixes A and B

These tables are limited to spellings and/or pronunciations occurring in the *American College Dictionary*,[1] which contains about 132,000 words (71,000 main entries); less than 30% of the 450,000 words in the best-known unabridged dictionary. Also, no proper names, however common, have been included.

To maintain a measure of consistency and eliminate duplicate counting of silent letters, *all consonant letters* except the semi-vowels *w, y,* and *h have been treated as part of the spelling of a consonant sound,* and *all vowel letters have been treated as part of the spelling of a vowel sound,* with only four exceptions:

Where their position in a word renders such treatment impossible — e.g., ch*oir*, q*uite*, thr*ough*, dep*ot*.

Where the silent letters *gh* follow a long vowel — e.g., str*aight*, m*ight*, c*aught*, b*ought*.

In some spellings of /ʃ/, /ʒ/, /č/, and /j/, where linguistically the grapheme for the consonant phoneme is considered to include a following *i* or *e* — e.g., na*ti*on, o*ce*an, mi*ssi*on, vi*si*on, que*sti*on, sol*di*er.

In the suffix *ed,* when pronounced /t/ or /d/; e.g., ask*ed,* call*ed.*

---

[1] The *American College Dictionary* was selected because, among current abridged dictionaries, its 43-sound pronunciation key comes nearest to a simple phonemic basis. For this study, that key has been further reduced to the 41-sound basis of the Simpler Spelling Association (SSA) phonemic alphabet (see page 34) by combining the vowel sounds of *age* and *air,* and the stressed and unstressed vowel sounds of *murmur.*

Appendix A

Spellings of sounds

Arrangement of spellings table

The 41 sounds are arranged in the order in which they appear in the SSA phonemic alphabet shown on page 34 — a logical and convenient order familiar to many students of shorthand. The spellings are arranged under each sound in the alphabetic order of the letters that spell the sound.

The heading for each sound is to be read: /p/ as heard in — pin cup — is spelled in 5 different ways in such words as . . . , etc.

This table lists only the spellings of *single sounds:* therefore, where one letter, such as x in next, represents two sounds, or two letters taken together, such as *oi* in memoir, represent two sounds each quite different from the normal value of the separate letter, or in a different order, as with the letters *wh* for the sounds /hw/, each of the separate sounds has been listed as spelled by $\frac{1}{2}$ of the combination; e.g., $\frac{1}{2}x$ as a spelling of /k/ and $\frac{1}{2}x$ as a spelling of /s/, etc.

For each spelling exemplified, the 4-line arrangement gives: on the first line, the conventionally spelled word; on the second, the letters of that word that spell the sound in question; on the third, the same word transcribed in the phonemically accurate notation of the SSA phonemic alphabet, substantiating the pronunciation; and on the fourth, the same word transcribed in the no-new-letter World English Spelling (WES) notation shown on page 30. WES forms (based on alternative pronunciations) which are not first choice are enclosed in ( ).

Spellings or pronunciations which are not the first choice of the *American College Dictionary* are identified by the subscript $_2$ (or $_3$ or $_4$) immediately following.

94

Spellings of sounds

p as heard in — *p*in cu*p* — is spelled in
5 different ways in such words as

hiccough	halfpenny	pay	naphtha
gh	lfp	p	ph
hikʊp	hɑpeni	pɑ	napꞃə
hikʊp	haepeni	pae	napthha

happy
pp
hapi
hapi

b as heard in — *b*in cu*b* — is spelled in
5 different ways in such words as

by	rubber	bhang	cupboard	hautboy
b	bb	bh	pb	tb
bɑ́	rʊbər	baŋ	kʊbərd	hobꞃ
bie	ruber	bang	kubord	hoeboi

t as heard in — *t*en be*t* — is spelled in
14 different ways in such words as

debt	yacht	indict	hoped	veldt	asked
bt	cht	ct	d	dt	ed
det	yɒt	indɑ́t	hopt	velt	askt
det	yot	indiet	hoept	velt	askt

phthisic	receipt	it	thyme
phth	pt	t	th
tizik	risɛt	it	tɑ́m
tizik	reseet	it	tiem

little	two	scherzo	pizzicato
tt	tw	$\frac{1}{2}$z	$\frac{1}{2}$zz
litəl	tuu	skertso	pitsəkɑto
litel	too	skertsoe	pitsikaatoe

d
7
as heard in — *d*en be*d* — is spelled in
different ways in such words as

bdellium	and	add	dhow	called
bd	d	dd	dh	ed
deli ʊm	and	ad	dɑɪ	kɔld
delium	and	ad	dou	kauld

would	mezzo
ld	z
wud	medzo
wuud	medzoe

k
17
as heard in — *c*ome ba*ck* — is spelled in
different ways in such words as

can	account	bacchanal	school	back
c	cc	cch	ch	ck
kan	əkaʊnt	bakənəl	skʉl	bak
kan	akount	bakanal	skool	bak

lacquer	lough	kind	khaki	falcon
cq	gh	k	kh	lc
lakər	lɒk	kɑɪnd	kaki	fɔkənₙ
laker	lok	kiend	kaki	(faukon)

talk	quite	forecastle	viscount	except
lk	q	reca	sc	x
tɔk	kwɑɪt	foksəl	vɑkaʊnt	iksept
tauk	kwiet	foeksel	viekount	eksept

next	noxious
½x	½xi
nekst	nɒkʃ ʊs
nekst	nokshus

g
6
as heard in — *g*um ba*g* — is spelled in
different ways in such words as

eczema	blackguard	good	egg	ghost	exact
c	ckg	g	gg	gh	½x
egzɛməₙ	blagɑrd	gud	eg	gost	igzakt
egzeema	blagard	guud	eg	goest	egzakt

f
8
as heard in — *f*an sa*f*e — is spelled in
different ways in such words as

for	off	often	enough	half	graphic
f	ff	ft	gh	lf	ph
fɔr	ɒf₂	ɒfən₂	inuf	haf	grafik
for	of	ofen	enuf	haf	grafik

sapphire	lieutenant
pph	u
safár	leftenənt₂
safier	(leftenant)

v
8
as heard in — *v*an sa*v*e — is spelled in
different ways in such words as

of	halve	nephew	view	we've	navvy
f	lv	ph	v	've	vv
ɒv	hav	neviʉ₂	viʉ	wɛ'v	navi
ov	hav	(nevue)	vue	wee'v	navi

schwa	rendezvous
w	zv
ʃvɑ₂	rɑndəvʉ
(shvaa)	raandevoo

ƕ
4
as heard in — *th*igh ba*th* — is spelled in
different ways in such words as

chthonian	eighth	phthisis	things
chth	h	phth	th
ƕoniən	atƕ	ƕásis	ƕiŋz
thhoenian	aetthh	thhiesis	thhingz

ƕ
2
as heard in — *th*y ba*the* — is spelled in
different ways in such words as

that	ye
th	y
ƕat	ƕɛ
that	the

s   as heard in — seal race — is spelled in
17   different ways in such words as

cent	psalm	worsted	this	scene
c	ps	rs	s	sc
sent	sɑm	wustid	ḣis	sɛn
sent	saam	wuusted	this	seen

schism	less	listen	isthmus	sword
sch	ss	st	sth	sw
sizəm	les	lisən	ismʊs	sord
sizem	les	lisen	ismus	sord

boatswain	xi_2	next	waltz	scherzo
tsw	x	$\frac{1}{2}x$	z	$\frac{1}{2}z$
bosən	sɑ́	nekst	wɔlts	skertso
boesen	sie	nekst	waults	skertsoe

britzska	pizzicato
zs	$\frac{1}{2}zz$
britskə	pitsəkɑto
britska	pitsikaatoe

ʑ   as heard in — zeal raise — is spelled in
13   different ways in such words as

czar	is	discern	housewife	business
cz	s	sc	sew	si
zɑr	iz	dizərn	hʊzif$_2$	biznis
zar	iz	dizurn	(huzif)	biznis

raspberry	scissors	asthma	clothes
sp	ss	sth	thes
razberi	sizərz	azmə	kloz
razberi	sizerz	azma	kloez

xylophone	exact	zone	puzzle
x	$\frac{1}{2}x$	z	zz
zɑ́ləfon	igzakt	zon	pʊzəl
zielofoen	egzakt	zoen	puzel

ʃ
20 as heard in—*sh*abby a*ss*ure ru*sh*—is spelled in different ways in such words as

oceanic	ocean	chaise	fuchsia	social
c	ce	ch	chsi	ci
oʃianik	oʃən	ʃaz	fiuʃə	soʃəl
oeshianik	oeshon	shaez	fuesha	soeshal

pshaw	sure	crescendo	schwa	conscience
psh	s	sc	sch	sci
ʃɔ	ʃur	krəʃendo	ʃwa	konʃəns
shau	shuur	kreshendoe	shwaa	konshens

nauseous	she	pension	ski	issue
se	sh	si	sk	ss
nɔʃəs	ʃɛ	penʃən	ʃɛ[2]	iʃɯ
naushus	shee	penshon	(shee)	ishoo

mission	negotiate	nation	luxury
ssi	t	ti	½x
miʃən	nigoʃiat	naʃən	lukʃəri
mishon	negoeshiaet	naeshon	luksheri

noxious
½xi
nɒkʃəs
nokshus

ʒ
10 as heard in—*j*abot a*z*ure rou*g*e—is spelled in different ways in such words as

rouge	jardiniere	pleasure	occasion
g	j	s	si
rɯʒ	ʒardɛnyere	pleʒər	əkaʒən
roozh	zhardeenyer	plezher	okaezhon

scission	equation	luxurious	azure
ssi	ti	½x	z
siʒən	ikwaʒən	lugʒuriəs	aʒər
sizhon	ekwaezhon	lugzhuurius	azher

brazier	muzjik[4]
zi	zj
braʒər	mɯʒik
braezher	moozhik

č as heard in — *ch*oke *ch*ur*ch* ri*ch* — is spelled in
7 different ways in such words as

cello	which	situation	match
c	ch	t	tch
čelo	hwič	sičuaʃən	mač
cheloe	which	sichuuaeshon	mach

righteous	posthumous	question
te	th	ti
ráčəs	pɒsčuməs	kwesčən
riechus	poschuumus	kweschon

j as heard in — *j*oke *j*ud*g*e ri*dg*e — is spelled in
12 different ways in such words as

spinach	education	grandeur	knowledge
ch	d	de	dg
spinij₂	ejukaʃən	granjər	nɒlij
(spinij)	ejuukaeshon	granjer	nolej

soldier	adjust	large	gorgeous
di	dj	g	ge
soljər	əjust	larj	gɔrjəs
soeljer	ajust	larj	gorjus

exaggerate	region	just	hajji
gg	gi	j	jj
igzajərat	rɛjən	just	haji
egzajeraet	reejon	just	haji

m as heard in — *m*et hi*m* — is spelled in
8 different ways in such words as

drachm	phlegm	palm	from	criticism
chm	gm	lm	m	½m
dram	flem	pɑm	frɒm	kritəsizəm
dram	flem	paam	from	kritisizem

lamb	common	hymn
mb	mm	mn
lam	kɒmən	him
lam	komon	him

n as heard in — *n*et thi*n* — is spelled in
14 different ways in such words as

studdingsail	gnaw	vignette	know
dding	gn	½gn	kn
stunsəl	nɔ	vinyet	no
stunsel	nau	vinyet	noe

mnemonic	comptroller	in	cañon
mn	mp	n	½ñ
nɛmɒnik	kəntrolər	in	kanyən
neemonik	kontroeler	in	kanyon

handsome	dinner	habitant	gunwale
nd	nn	nt	nw
hansəm	dinər	abɛtan₂	gunəl
hansum	diner	(aabeetaan)	gunel

pneumatic	demesne
pn	sn
niumatik	dimɑn
nuematik	demaen

ŋ as heard in — i*n*k thi*ng* — is spelled in
3 different ways in such words as

think	handkerchief	thing
n	nd	ng
ƕiŋk	haŋkərčif	ƕiŋ
thhink	hankerchif	thhing

l as heard in — *l*aid dea*l* — is spelled in
7 different ways in such words as

muscle	intaglio	like	people	all
cl	gl	l	½le	ll
musəl	intɑlyo	lɑ́k	pɛpəl	ɔl
musel	intaalyoe	liek	peepel	aul

kiln	island
ln	sl
kil	ɑ́lənd
kil	ieland

r   as heard in – *r*aid dea*r* – is spelled in
11   different ways in such words as

colonel	for	they're	centre	rhyme	corps
l	r	're	$\frac{1}{2}$re	rh	rps
kərnəl	fɔr	ħa'r	sentər	rɑ́m	kor
kurnel	for	thae'r	senter	riem	kor

carry	myrrh	hors d'oeuvre	mortgage	write
rr	rrh	rs	rt	wr
kari	mər	ɔr d'ərv	mɔrgij	rɑ́t
karri	mur	or d'urv	morgej	riet

w   as heard in – *w*et *w*e – is spelled in
10   different ways in such words as

choir	one	memoir	repertoire	patois
o	$\frac{1}{2}$o-e	$\frac{1}{2}$oi	$\frac{1}{2}$oi-e	$\frac{1}{2}$ois
kwɑ́r	wun	memwar	repərtwar	patwɑ
kwier	wun	memwar	repertwar	patwaa

bivouac	quite	with	whelk	when
ou	u	w	wh	$\frac{1}{2}$wh
bivwak	kwɑ́t	wiħ	wilk₂	hwen
bivwak	kwiet	with	(wilk)	when

y   as heard in – *y*et *y*e – is spelled in
8   different ways in such words as

azalea	vignette	union	hallelujah
e	$\frac{1}{2}$gn	i	j
əzalyə	vinyet	iunyən	haləluɪyə
azaelya	vinyet	uenyon	halelooya

bouillon	tortilla	cañon	yet
l	ll	$\frac{1}{2}$ñ	y
bulyɒn	tɔrtɛya	kanyən	yet
buulyon	torteeyaa	kanyon	yet

h   as heard in – *h*ead *h*e – is spelled in
3   different ways in such words as

his	who	which
h	wh	$\frac{1}{2}$wh
hiz	huɪ	hwiċ
hiz	hoo	which

a
13 as heard in — *a*m p*a*t — is spelled in different ways in such words as

had	ma'am	have	baa	hae	dahlia
a	a'a	a-e	aa	ae	ah
had	mam	hav	ba	ha$_2$	dalyə
had	mam	hav	ba	(ha)	dalya

plaid	laugh	harangue	lingerie
ai	au	a - ue	i
plad	laf	həraŋ	lanʒərɛ$_2$
plad	laf	harang	(lanzheree)

meringue	guarantee	guimpe
i - ue	ua	ui - e
məraŋ	garəntɛ	gamp$_2$
merang	garrantee	(gamp)

ɑ
16 as heard in — *a*lms p*a*rt m*a* — is spelled in different ways in such words as

part	ma'am	bazaar	are	ah	eclat
a	a'a	aa	a-e	ah	at
part	mam$_2$	bəzar	ɑr	ɑ	aklɑ
part	(maam)	bazar	ar	aa	aeklaa

taunt	barque$_2$	sergeant	heart	habitant
au	a - ue	e	ea	ha
tɑnt$_2$	bɑrk	sɑrjənt	hɑrt	abɛtɑn$_2$
(taant)	bark	sarjant	hart	(aabeetaan)

lingerie	memoir	repertoire	patois
i	½oi	oi-e	½ois
lanʒərɑ	memwɑr	repərtwɑr	patwɑ
laanzherae	memwar	repertwar	patwaa

guard
ua
gɑrd
gard

e as heard in — *e*dge l*e*t — is spelled in
19 different ways in such words as

many	ate	diaerisis	said	says	men
a	a-e	ae	ai	ay	e
meni	et₂	dáerəsis	sed	sez	men
meni	(et)	die.erisis	sed	sez	men

ledge	head	cleanse	keelson	belles-lettres
e - e	ea	ea - e	ee	e - es
lej	hed	klenz	kelsən	bel-letr
lej	hed	klenz	kelson	bel-letr

eh	heifer	leopard	cheque₂	friend
eh	ei	eo	e - ue	ie
e₂	hefər	lepərd	ćek	frend
(e)	hefer	lepard	chek	frend

foetid₂	bury	guess
oe	u	ue
fetid	beri	ges
fetid	beri	ges

a as heard in — *a*ge l*a*te m*ay* *ai*r — is spelled in
36 different ways in such words as

making	made	maelstrom	dahlia	main
a	a-e	ae	ah	ai
makiŋ	mad	malstrəm	dalyə₃	man
maeking	maed	maelstrom	(daelya)	maen

raise	straight	gaol	plaguing	plague
ai-e	aigh	ao	a-u	a-ue
raz	strat	jal	plagiŋ	plag
raez	straet	jael	plaeging	plaeg

gauging	gauge	may	aye₂	mayor	re
au	au-e	ay	aye	ayo	e
gajiŋ	gaj	ma	a	mar₂	ra
gaejing	gaej	mae	ae	(maer)	rae

attaché	there	fête₂	e'er	great
é	e-e	ê-e	e'e	ea
atəʃa	har	fat	ar	grat
atashae	thaer	faet	aer	graet

matinee₂	matinée	eh	their	seine
ee	ée	eh	ei	ei-e
matəna	matəna	a	ħar	san
matinae	matinae	ae	thaer	saen

weigh	dossier	ballet	they	eyre
eigh	er	et	ey	ey-e
wa	dɒsia	bala	ħa	ɑr
wae	dosiae	balae	thae	aer

eyot	heir	lingerie	appliqué	bouquet
eyo	hei	ie	ué	uet
at₂	ar	lɑnʒɑra	aplika	bokɑ
(aet)	aer	laanzherae	aplikae	boekae

i as heard in — *is sit army* — is spelled in
33 different ways in such words as

imaging	image	caesura	shillelagh
a	a-e	ae	agh
imijiŋ	imij	siʒurə	ʃilali₂
imejing	imej	sizhuura	(shilaeli)

mountain	yesterday	pretty	guinea
ai	ay	e	ea
mɑuntin₂	yestərdi	priti	gini
(mountin)	(yesterdi)	priti	gini

college	been	forehead	forfeit
e-e	ee	ehea	ei
kɒlij	bin	fɔrid	fɔrfit
kolej	bin	fored	forfit

billet doux	money	exhibit	in	give
et	ey	hi	i	i-e
bili du	mʊni	igzibit	in	giv
bili doo	muni	egzibit	in	giv

bisque	marriages	marriage	carried
i-ue	ia	ia-e	ie
bisk	marijiz	marij	karid
bisk	marrejez	marrej	karrid

sieve	chassis	petit	women	chamois
ie-e	is	it	o	ois
siv	ʃasi	peti	wimin	ʃami
siv	shasi	peti	wimen	shami

busy	minute	plaguey₂	built	plaguy
u	u-e	uey	ui	uy
bizi	minit	plɑgi	bilt	plɑgi
bizi	minit	plaegi	bilt	plaegi

any	apocalypse
y	y - e
eni	əpɒkəlips
eni	apokalips

ɛ   as heard in — *ea*se s*ea*t m*e* — is spelled in
23   different ways in such words as

aeon	be	these	e'en	each	leave
ae	e	e-e	e'e	ea	ea-e
ɛən	bɛ	ħɛz	ɛn	ɛc̆	lɛv
eeon	bee	theez	een	eech	leev

league	see	cheese	receipt	receive
ea-ue	ee	ee-e	ei	ei-e
lɛg	sɛ	c̆ɛz	risɛt	risɛv
leeg	see	cheez	reseet	reseev

people	key	si	marine	antique
eo	ey	i	i-e	i-ue
pɛpəl	kɛ	sɛ	mərɛn	antɛk
peepel	kee	see	mareen	anteek

grief	believe	debris	esprit	amoeba
ie	ie-e	is	it	oe
grɛf	bilɛv	dəbrɛ	esprɛ	əmɛbə
greef	beleev	debree	espree	ameeba

quay	mosquito
uay	ui
kɛ	məskɛto
kee	moskeetoe

ɒ **11** as heard in — *o*dd n*o*t — is spelled in different ways in such words as

was	laurel	because	bureaucracy	honor
a	au	au-e	eau	ho
wɒz	lɒrəl₂	bikɒz₂	biurɒkrəsi	ɒnər
woz	(lorrel)	(bekoz)	buerokrasi	oner

of	gone	catalogue	demijohn	lough
o	o-e	o-ue	oh	ou
ɒv	gɒn₂	katəlɒg₂	demijɒn	lɒk
ov	gon	katalog	demijon	lok

knowledge
ow
nɒlij
nolej

ɔ **17** as heard in — *aw*ed n*augh*t psh*aw* — is spelled in different ways in such words as

fall	false	hurrah	extraordinary	haul
a	a-e	ah	ao	au
fɔl	fɔls	hərɔ₂	ikstrɔrdəneri	hɔl
faul	fauls	(herau)	ekstrordinari	haul

because	taught	saw	awe	exhaust
au-e	augh	aw	awe	hau
bikɔz	tɔt	sɔ	ɔ	igzɔst
bekauz	taut	sau	au	egzaust

hors d'oeuvre	for	gone	torque	broad
ho	o	o-e	o-ue	oa
ɔr d'arv	fɔr	gɒn	tɔrk	brɔd
or d'urv	for	(gaun)	tork	braud

memoir	thought
½oi	ough
memwɔr₂	ʃɔt
(memwor)	thhaut

ʊ
13

as heard in—ʊp tɒn—is spelled in
different ways in such words as

tam-tam	because	humble	other	some
a a	au-e	hu	o	o - e
tʊm-tʊm	bikʊz₃	ʊmbəl₂	ʊħər	sʊm
tum-tum	(bekuz)	(umbel)	uther	sum

one	tongue	does	flood	country	but
½o-e	o - ue	oe	oo	ou	u
wʊn	tʊŋ	dʊz	flʊd	kʊntri	bʊt
wun	tung	duz	flud	kuntri	but

judge	brusque
u - e	u - ue
jʊj	brʊsk
juj	brusk

o
23

as heard in—open tone show—is spelled in
different ways in such words as

chauffeur	mauve	beau	yeoman	sew
au	au-e	eau	eo	ew
ʃofər	mov	bo	yomən	so
shoefer	moev	boe	yoeman	soe

mustachio	no	more	o'er	rogue	coal
io	o	o-e	o'e	o-ue	oa
mʊstaʃo	no	mor	or	rog	kol
mustaashoe	noe	mor	or	roeg	koel

coarse	toe	oh	floor	apropos	depot
oa - e	oe	oh	oo	os	ot
kors	to	o	flor	aprəpo	dɛpo
kors	toe	oe	flor	apropoe	deepoe

four	course	though	know	toward	owe
ou	ou - e	ough	ow	owa	owe
for	kors	ħo	no	tord	o
for	kors	thoe	noe	tord	oe

u
12

as heard in — f**u**ll sh**ou**ld — is spelled in
different ways in such words as

pleurisy	silhouette	woman	good	pooh
eu	hou	o	oo	ooh
plurəsi	siluet	wumən	gud	pu₂
pluurisi	siluu.et	wuuman	guud	(puu)

should	bouillon	full	sure	brusque
ou	oui	u	u-e	u - ue
ʃud	bulyɒn	ful	ʃur	brusk₂
shuud	buulyon	fuul	shuur	(bruusk)

tissue	pugh
ue	ugh
tiʃu	pu₂
tishuu	(puu)

ɯ
29

as heard in — f**oo**l sh**oe**d sh**oe** — is spelled in
different ways in such words as

caoutchouc	leeward	rheum	crew	lieu
aou	eew	eu	ew	ieu
kuɯcuk	luərd	ruɯm	kruɯ	luɯ
koochuuk	looard	room	kroo	loo

do	move	shoe	manoeuvre₂	too	loose
o	o-e	oe	oeu	oo	oo-e
duɯ	muɯv	ʃuɯ	mənuɯvər	tuɯ	luɯs
doo	moov	shoo	manoover	too	loos

pooh	soup	route	denouement	through
ooh	ou	ou-e	oue	ough
puɯ	suɯp	ruɯt	dənuɯmɑn	ħruɯ
poo	soop	root	denoomaan	thhroo

brougham	coup	rendezvous	ragout
ougha	oup	ous	out
brum₂	kuɯp	rɑndəvuɯ	raguɯ
(broom)	koop	raandevoo	ragoo

billet-doux	truly	rule	true	pugh
oux	u	u-e	ue	ugh
bili-duɯ	truɯli	ruɯl	truɯ	puɯ
bili-doo	trooli	rool	troo	poo

buhl	fruit	bruise	buoy
uh	ui	ui-e	uo
buul	fruut	bruuz	buui$_2$
bool	froot	brooz	(booy)

ə as heard in — *a*bout f*u*rther dat*a* — is spelled in
43 different ways: 36 unstressed, 16 stressed, 9 both.
Stressed examples are distinguished by *; those which
duplicate unstressed examples are enclosed in ( ), and
are not counted as additional spellings.

about	nuisance	shillelagh	sirrah	mountain
a	a - e	agh	ah	ai
əbaut	niusəns	ʃilalə	sirə	mauntən
about	nuesans	shilaela	sira	mounten

blanc-mange	restaurant	over	(her*)
anc	au	e	e
blə-manʒ	restərənt	ovər	hər
bla-maanzh	restarant	oever	hur

license	(were*)	early*	hearse*	mullein
e - e	e-e	ea	ea - e	ei
láisəns	wər	ərli	hərs	mulən
liesens	wur	urli	hurs	mulen

luncheon	connoisseur*	gingham	herb*
eo	eu	ha	he
lunʹcən	kɒnəsər	giŋəm	ərb
lunchon	konisur	gingam	urb

vehicle	elixir	(first*)	engine	iron
hi	i	i	i-e	½i-o
vɛəkəl	iliksər	fərst	enjən	áiərn
veeikel	eliksir	furst	enjin	ie.ern

parliament	mischievous	fashion	people
ia	ie	io	½le
parləmənt	misʹcəvəs	faʃən	pɛpəl
parlament	mischevus	fashon	peepel

criticism	labor	(world*)	welcome
½m	o	o	o - e
kritəsizəm	labər	wərld	welkəm
kritisizem	laebor	wurld	welkom

(worse*)   colonel*   cupboard   avoirdupois
o - e   o-o   oa   oi
wərs   kərnəl   kubərd   avərdəpɔiz
wurs   kurnel   kubord   averdupoiz

porpoise   glamour   (journey*)   scourge*
oi-e   ou   ou   ou - e
pɔrpəs   glamər   jərni   skərj
porpus   glamor   jurni   skurj

bellows   centre₂   sulphur   (turn*)   pleasure
ow   ½re   u   u   u-e
beləs₂   sentər   sulfər   tərn   pleʒər
(belos)   senter   sulfer   turn   plezher

piquant   lacquer   (guerdon*)   liqueur*
ua   ue   ue   ueu
pɛkənt   lakər   gərdən   likər
peekant   laker   gurdon   likur

buhr*   liquor   martyr   (myrrh*)
uh   uo   y   y
bər   likər   martər   mər
bur   liker   marter   mur

á   as heard in—*ai*sle p*i*nt b*y*—is spelled in
22 different ways in such words as

assegai   aisle   ay   aye   stein   height
ai   ai - e   ay   aye   ei   eigh
asəgá   ál   á   á   stán   hát
asegie   iel   ie   ie   stien   hiet

eying   eye   kind   time   oblique   iron
ey   eye   i   i - e   i-ue   ½i-o
áiŋ   á   kánd   tám   əblák₂   áərn
ieing   ie   kiend   tiem   (obliek)   ie.ern

diamond   lie   high   coyote   guiding
ia   ie   igh   oy   ui
dámənd   lá   há   káot   gádiŋ
diemond   lie   hie   kieoet   gieding

guide   buy   by   type   dye
ui-e   uy   y   y-e   ye
gád   bá   bá   táp   dá
gied   bie   bie   tiep   die

aʊ   as heard in — *owl* p*ou*nd b*ough* — is spelled in
7   different ways in such words as

caoutchouc	umlaut	hour	out	house
aou		au	hou	ou	ou-e
kaʊc̆uuk₂	umlaʊt	aʊr	aʊt	haʊs
(kouchook)	uumlout	our	out	hous

bough	now
ough	ow
baʊ	naʊ
bou	nou

ɔɪ   as heard in — *oil* p*oi*nt b*oy* — is spelled in
7   different ways in such words as

point	noise	boys	gargoyle	quoin
oi	oi-e	oy	oy-e	uoi
pɔɪnt	nɔɪz	bɔɪz	gɑrgɔɪl	kɔɪn
point	noiz	boiz	gargoil	koin

turquoise	buoy
uoi-e	uoy
tərkɔɪz	bɔɪ
turkoiz	boi

ɪu   as heard in — *u*sed *you*r p*u*re d*ue* — is spelled in
18   different ways in such words as

beauty	feod₂	feud	deuce	few	ewe
eau	eo	eu	eu-e	ew	ewe
bɪuti	fɪud	fɪud	dɪus	fɪu	ɪu
bueti	fued	fued	dues	fue	ue

humor	view	during	use	fugue	due
hu	iew	u	u-e	u-ue	ue
ɪumər₂	vɪu	dɪurɪŋ	ɪuz	fɪug	dɪu
(uemor)	vue	duering	uez	fueg	due

queue	suit	debut	yew	you	yule
ueue	ui	ut	yew	you	yu-e
kɪu	sɪut	dibɪu	ɪu	ɪu	ɪul
kue	suet	debue	ue	ue	uel

Pronunciations of spellings

Arrangement of pronunciations table

The spellings of the 41 single sounds which appear in the preceding table are here rearranged in alphabetic order, in three groups: single letters, simple digraphs, and all other combinations of letters to represent a single sound. The pronunciations of each spelling are arranged in the order of their appearance in the table of spellings, which is the order of the SSA phonemic alphabet shown on page 34.

The heading for each spelling is to be read: *a* is pronounced 9 ways in . . . , etc.

This table, like the table of spellings of sounds on which it is based, lists only the spellings of *single sounds*. See therefore the note of explanation on page 94 with respect to such examples as $\frac{1}{2}x$ as a spelling of /k/ and $\frac{1}{2}x$ as a spelling of /s/, etc.

For each pronunciation exemplified, the 4-line arrangement gives: on the first line, the conventionally spelled word; on the second, the phonemic character for the pronunciation in question; on the third, the same word transcribed in the phonemically accurate notation of the SSA phonemic alphabet, substantiating the pronunciation; and on the fourth, the same word transcribed in the no-new-letter World English Spelling (WES) notation shown on page 30. WES forms (based on alternative pronunciations) which are not first choice are enclosed in ( ).

As in the table of spellings, spellings or pronunciations which are not the first choice of the *American College Dictionary* are identified by the subscript $_2$ (or $_3$ or $_4$) immediately following.

114

Single letters

a 9	is pronounced⎫ ways in ⎭	had	part	many
		a	ɑ	e
		had	pɑrt	meni
		had	part	meni

making	imaging	was	fall	tam-tam
a	i	ɒ	ɔ	ʊ ʊ
makiŋ	imijiŋ	wɒz	fɔl	tʊm-tʊm
maeking	imejing	woz	faul	tum-tum

about
ə
əbaut
about

b 1	is pronounced⎫ way in ⎭	by
		b
		bá
		bie

c 5	is pronounced⎫ ways in ⎭	can	eczema	cent
		k	g	s
		kan	egzɛmə₂	sent
		kan	egzeema	sent

oceanic	cello
ʃ	č
oʃianik	čelo
oeshianik	cheloe

d 3	is pronounced⎫ ways in ⎭	hoped	and	education
		t	d	j
		hopt	and	ejukaʃən
		hoept	and	ejuukaeshon

e 7	is pronounced⎫ ways in ⎭	azalea	sergeant	men
		y	ɑ	e
		əzɑlyə	sarjənt	men
		azaelya	sarjant	men

re	pretty	be	over	(her*)
ɑ	i	ɛ	ə	ə
rɑ	priti	bɛ	ovər	hər
rae	priti	bee	oever	hur

		for	of	
f	is pronounced	for	of	
2	ways in	f	v	
		fɔr	ɒv	
		for	ov	

		good	rouge	large
g	is pronounced	good	rouge	large
3	ways in	g	ʒ	j
		gud	ruʒ	lɑrj
		guud	roozh	larj

		eighth	his
h	is pronounced	eighth	his
2	ways in	ħ	h
		ɑtħ	hiz
		aetthh	hiz

		union	lingerie
i	is pronounced	union	lingerie
7	ways in	y	a
		ɯnyən	lanʒərɛ₂
		uenyon	(lanzheree)

lingerie	in	si	elixir
ɑ	i	ɛ	ə
lanʒərɑ	in	sɛ	iliksər
laanzherae	in	see	eliksir

(first*)	kind
ə	á
fərst	kánd
furst	kiend

		jardiniere	just	hallelujah
j	is pronounced	jardiniere	just	hallelujah
3	ways in	ʒ	j	y
		ʒɑrdɛnyer₂	jʊst	haləlɯyə
		zhardeenyer	just	halelooya

k	is pronounced⎫	kind
1	way in ⎭	k
		kȧnd
		kiend

l	is pronounced⎫	like	colonel	bouillon
3	ways in ⎭	l	r	y
		lȧk	kərnəl	bulyɒn
		liek	kurnel	buulyon

m	is pronounced⎫	from
1	way in ⎭	m
		frɒm
		from

n	is pronounced⎫	in	think
2	ways in ⎭	n	ŋ
		in	ḥiŋk
		in	thhink

o	is pronounced⎫	choir	women	of	for
9	ways in ⎭	w	i	ɒ	ɔ
		kwȧr	wimin	ɒv	fɔr
		kwier	wimen	ov	for

other	no	woman	do	labor
ʊ	o	u	ɯ	ə
ʊḥər	no	wumən	duu	labər
uther	noe	wuuman	doo	laebor

(world*)

ə

wərld

wurld

p	is pronounced⎫	pay
1	way in ⎭	p
		pɑ
		pae

q	is pronounced ⎱	quite
1	way in ⎰	k
		kwᴀt
		kwiet

r	is pronounced ⎱	for
1	way in ⎰	r
		fɔr
		for

s	is pronounced ⎱	this	is	sure	pleasure
4	ways in ⎰	s	z	ʃ	ʒ
		ħis	iz	ʃur	pleʒər
		this	iz	shuur	plezher

t	is pronounced ⎱	it	negotiate	situation
3	ways in ⎰	t	ʃ	ċ
		it	nigoʃiat	sicuaʃən
		it	negoeshiaet	sichuuaeshon

u	is pronounced ⎱	lieutenant	quite	bury
9	ways in ⎰	f	w	e
		leftenənt₂	kwᴀt	beri
		(leftenant)	kwiet	beri

busy	but	full	truly	sulphur
i	ʊ	u	ɯ	ə
bizi	bʊt	ful	truɯli	sulfər
bizi	but	fuul	trooli	sulfer

(turn*)	during
ə	iu
tərn	diuriŋ
turn	duering

v	is pronounced ⎱	view
1	way in ⎰	v
		viu
		vue

w	is pronounced⎫	schwa	with
2	ways in ⎭	v	w
		ʃvɑ₂	wiħ
		(shvaa)	with

As representing a single sound,

x	is pronounced⎫	except	xi	xylophone
3	ways in ⎭	k	s	z
		iksept	sɑ₂	zɑləfon
		eksept	sie	zielofoen

As representing two sounds, *x* is pronounced in several additional ways, tabulated and counted under $\frac{1}{2}x$ and $\frac{1}{2}xi$ on p. 155.

y	is pronounced⎫	ye	yet	any	martyr
5	ways in ⎭	ħ	y	i	ə
		ħɛ	yet	eni	mɑrtər
		the	yet	eni	marter

(myrrh*)	by
ə	ɑ́
mər	bɑ́
mur	bie

z	is pronounced⎫	mezzo	waltz	zone
4	ways in ⎭	d	s	z
		medzo	wɔlts	zon
		medzoe	waults	zoen

azure
ʒ
aʒər
azher

Summary

51 pronunciations/21 consonants = 2.4 per letter
41 pronunciations/ 5 vowels = 8.2 per letter
92 pronunciations/26 letters = 3.5 per letter

Simple digraphs

aa
2 is pronounced ⎫
ways in ⎭

baa	bazaar
a	ɑ
ba	bəzɑr
ba	bazar

ae
5 is pronounced ⎫
ways in ⎭

hae	diaerisis₂	maelstrom
a	e	ɑ
ha₂	dɑerəsis	mɑlstrəm
(ha)	die.erisis	maelstrom

caesura	aeon
i	ɛ
siʒurə	ɛən
sizhuura	eeon

ah
5 is pronounced ⎫
ways in ⎭

dahlia	ah	dahlia
a	ɑ	ɑ
dalyə	ɑ	dɑlyə₃
dalya	aa	(daelya)

hurrah	sirrah
ɔ	ə
hərɔ₂	sirə
(herau)	sira

ai
6 is pronounced ⎫
ways in ⎭

plaid	said	main
a	e	ɑ
plad	sed	mɑn
plad	sed	maen

mountain	mountain	assegai
i	ə	á
mɑntin₂	mɑntən	asəgá
(mountin)	mounten	asegie

ao
2 is pronounced ⎫
ways in ⎭

gaol	extraordinary
ɑ	ɔ
jɑl	ikstrɔrdəneri
jael	ekstrordinari

at	is pronounced⎫	eclat
1	way in ⎭	ɑ
		aklɑ
		aeklaa

au	is pronounced⎫	laugh	taunt	gauging
8	ways in ⎭	a	ɑ	a
		laf	tɑnt₂	gajiŋ
		laf	(taant)	gaejing

laurel	haul	chauffeur	restaurant
ɒ	ɔ	o	ə
lɒrəl₂	hɔl	ʃofər	restərənt
(lorrel)	haul	shoefer	restarant

umlaut
   ɑʊ
umlaʊt
uumlout

aw	is pronounced⎫	saw
1	way in ⎭	ɔ
		sɔ
		sau

ay	is pronounced⎫	says	may	yesterday	ay
4	ways in ⎭	e	a	i	á
		sez	ma	yestərdi	á
		sez	mae	(yesterdi)	ie

bb	is pronounced⎫	rubber
1	way in ⎭	b
		rʊbər
		ruber

bd	is pronounced⎫	bdellium
1	way in ⎭	d
		deliʊm
		delium

bh	is pronounced⎫	bhang
1	way in ⎭	b
		baŋ
		bang

bt	is pronounced⎫	debt
1	way in ⎭	t
		det
		det

cc	is pronounced⎫	account
1	way in ⎭	k
		əkaʊnt
		akount

ce	is pronounced⎫	ocean
1	way in ⎭	ʃ
		oʃən
		oeshan

ch	is pronounced⎫	school	chaise	which
4	ways in ⎭	k	ʃ	č
		skul	ʃɑz	hwič
		skool	shaez	which

spinach
j
spinij₂
(spinij)

ci	is pronounced⎫	social
1	way in ⎭	ʃ
		soʃəl
		soeshal

ck	is pronounced⎫	back
1	way in ⎭	k
		bak
		bak

cl	is pronounced⎫	muscle
l	way in ⎭	l
		musəl
		musel

cq	is pronounced⎫	lacquer
l	way in ⎭	k
		lakər
		laker

ct	is pronounced⎫	indict
l	way in ⎭	t
		indát
		indiet

cz	is pronounced⎫	czar
l	way in ⎭	z
		zɑr
		zar

dd	is pronounced⎫	add
l	way in ⎭	d
		ad
		ad

de	is pronounced⎫	grandeur
l	way in ⎭	j
		granjər
		granjer

dg	is pronounced⎫	knowledge
l	way in ⎭	j
		nɒlij
		nolej

dh	is pronounced⎫	dhow
l	way in ⎭	d
		dau
		dou

di   is pronounced ⎫   soldier
1   way in   ⎭   j
                                        soljər
                                        soeljer

dj   is pronounced ⎫   adjust
1   way in   ⎭   j
                                          ajʊst
                                          ajust

dt   is pronounced ⎫   veldt
1   way in   ⎭   t
                                          velt
                                          velt

ea   is pronounced ⎫   heart   head   great
6   ways in   ⎭   ɑ   e   ɑ
                                          hɑrt   hed   grɑt
                                          hart   hed   graet

          guinea   each   early*
              i   ɛ   ə
          gini   ɛc   ərli
          gini   eech   urli

ed   is pronounced ⎫   asked   called
2   ways in   ⎭   t   d
                                          askt   kɔld
                                          askt   kauld

ee   is pronounced ⎫   keelson   matinee₂   been
4   ways in   ⎭   e   ɑ   i
                                          kelsən   matəna   bin
                                          kelson   matinae   bin

          see
            ɛ
          sɛ
          see

eh	is pronounced⎫	eh	eh	
2	ways in ⎭	e	ɑ	
		e₂	ɑ	
		(e)	ae	

ei	is pronounced⎫	heifer	their	forfeit
6	ways in ⎭	e	ɑ	i
		hefər	hɑr	fɔrfit
		hefer	thaer	forfit

	receipt	mullein	stein
	ɛ	ə	ȧ
	risɛt	mʊlən	stȧn
	reseet	mulen	stien

eo	is pronounced⎫	leopard	people	yeoman
5	ways in ⎭	e	ɛ	o
		lepərd	pɛpəl	yomən
		lepard	peepel	yoeman

	luncheon	feod₂
	ə	ɪʉ
	lʊnčən	fɪʉd
	lunchon	fued

er	is pronounced⎫	dossier
1	way in ⎭	ɑ
		dɒsiɑ
		dosiae

et	is pronounced⎫	ballet	billet doux
2	ways in ⎭	ɑ	i
		bɑlɑ	bili dʉ
		balae	bili doo

eu	is pronounced⎫	pleurisy	rheum
4	ways in ⎭	u	ɯ
		plurəsi	rɯm
		pluurisi	room

connoisseur*   feud
        ə   ɯ
kɒnəsər   fɯd
konisur   fued

ew   is pronounced ⎫   sew   crew   few
3   ways in   ⎭   o   ɯ   ɯ
                               so   krɯ   fɯ
                               soe   kroo   fue

ey   is pronounced ⎫   they   money   key   eying
4   ways in   ⎭   a   i   ɛ   á
                               ħa   mʊni   kɛ   áiŋ
                               thae   muni   kee   ieing

ff   is pronounced ⎫   off
1   way in   ⎭   f
                               ɒf₂
                               of

ft   is pronounced ⎫   often
1   way in   ⎭   f
                               ɒfən n₂
                               ofen

ge   is pronounced ⎫   gorgeous
1   way in   ⎭   j
                               gɔrjəs
                               gorjus

gg   is pronounced ⎫   egg   exaggerate
2   ways in   ⎭   g   j
                               eg   igzajərat
                               eg   egzajeraet

gh   is pronounced ⎫   hiccough   lough   ghost
4   ways in   ⎭   p   k   g
                               hikʊp   lɒk   gost
                               hikup   lok   goest

enough
f
inuf
enuf

gi 1	is pronounced} way in	region j rɛjən reejon	

gl 1	is pronounced} way in	intaglio l intɑlyo intaalyoe	

gm 1	is pronounced} way in	phlegm m flem flem	

gn 1	is pronounced} way in	gnaw n nɔ nau	

ha 2	is pronounced} ways in	habitant ɑ ɑbɛtɑn$_2$ (aabeetaan)	gingham ə giŋəm gingam

he 1	is pronounced} way in	herb* ə ərb urb	

hi 2	is pronounced} ways in	exhibit i igzibit egzibit	vehicle ə vɛəkəl veeikel

ho is pronounced⎤ honor   hors d'oeuvre
2   ways in   ⎦ ɒ   ɔ
                            ɒnər   ɔr d'arv
                            onor   or d'urv

hu is pronounced⎤ humble   humor
2   ways in   ⎦ ʊ   iu
                            ʊmbəl$_2$ iumər$_2$
                            (umbel) (uemor)

ia is pronounced⎤ marriages parliament
3   ways in   ⎦ i   ə
                            marijiz   pɑrləmənt
                            marrejez parlament

          diamond
          ɑ́
          dɑ́mənd
          diemond

ie is pronounced⎤ friend   lingerie   carried
6   ways in   ⎦ e   ɑ   i
                            frend   lɑnʒəra   karid
                            frend   laanzherae carrid

   grief   mischievous   lie
   ɛ   ə   ɑ́
   grɛf   misɕəvəs   lɑ́
   greef   mischevus   lie

io is pronounced⎤ mustachio fashion
2   ways in   ⎦ o   ə
                            mʊstaʃo   faʃən
                            mustaashoe fashon

is is pronounced⎤ chassis   debris
2   ways in   ⎦ i   ɛ
                            ʃasi   dəbrɛ
                            shasi   debree

it	is pronounced⎱	petit	esprit
2	ways in ⎰	i	ɛ
		peti	esprɛ
		peti	espree

jj	is pronounced⎱	hajji	
1	way in ⎰	j	
		haji	
		haji	

kh	is pronounced⎱	khaki	
1	way in ⎰	k	
		kaki	
		kaki	

kn	is pronounced⎱	know	
1	way in ⎰	n	
		no	
		noe	

lc	is pronounced⎱	falcon	
1	way in ⎰	k	
		fɔkən$_2$	
		(faukon)	

ld	is pronounced⎱	would	
1	way in ⎰	d	
		wud	
		wuud	

lf	is pronounced⎱	half	
1	way in ⎰	f	
		haf	
		haf	

lk	is pronounced⎱	talk	
1	way in ⎰	k	
		tɔk	
		tauk	

ll	is pronounced⎫	all	tortilla
2	ways in ⎬	l	y
	⎭	ɔl	tɔrtɛyɑ
		aul	torteeyaa

lm	is pronounced⎫	palm
1	way in ⎬	m
	⎭	pɑm
		paam

ln	is pronounced⎫	kiln
1	way in ⎬	l
	⎭	kil
		kil

lv	is pronounced⎫	halve
1	way in ⎬	v
	⎭	hav
		hav

mb	is pronounced⎫	lamb
1	way in ⎬	m
	⎭	lam
		lam

mm	is pronounced⎫	common
1	way in ⎬	m
	⎭	kɒmən
		komon

mn	is pronounced⎫	hymn	mnemonic
2	ways in ⎬	m	n
	⎭	him	nɛmɒnik
		him	neemonik

mp	is pronounced⎫	comptroller
1	way in ⎬	n
	⎭	kəntrolər
		kontroeler

nd	is pronounced⎤	handsome	handkerchief
2	ways in ⎦	n	ŋ
		hansəm	haŋkərćif
		hansom	hankerchif

ng	is pronounced⎤	thing
1	way in ⎦	ŋ
		ħiŋ
		thhing

nn	is pronounced⎤	dinner
1	way in ⎦	n
		dinər
		diner

nt	is pronounced⎤	habitant
1	way in ⎦	n
		abɛtɑn₂
		(aabeetaan)

nw	is pronounced⎤	gunwale
1	way in ⎦	n
		gunəl
		gunel

oa	is pronounced⎤	broad	coal	cupboard
3	ways in ⎦	ɔ	o	ə
		brɔd	kol	kubərd
		braud	koel	kubord

oe	is pronounced⎤	foetid₂	amoeba	does
5	ways in ⎦	e	ɛ	ʊ
		fetid	əmɛbə	dʊz
		fetid	ameeba	dʊz

	toe	shoe
	o	ɯ
	to	ʃɯ
	toe	shoo

oh   is pronounced⎫   demijohn   oh
2   ways in   ⎬   ɒ   o
    ⎭   demijɒn   o
       demijon   oe

oi   is pronounced⎫   avoirdupois   point
2   ways in   ⎬   ə   ɔ
       avərdəpɔz   pɔnt
       averdupoiz   point

oo   is pronounced⎫   flood   floor   good   too
4   ways in   ⎬   ʊ   o   u   ɯ
       flʊd   flor   gud   tɯ
       flud   flor   guud   too

os   is pronounced⎫   apropos
1   way in   ⎬   o
       aprəpo
       apropoe

ot   is pronounced⎫   depot
1   way in   ⎬   o
       dɛpo
       deepoe

ou   is pronounced⎫   bivouac   lough   country
8   ways in   ⎬   w   ɒ   ʊ
       bivwak   lɒk   kʊntri
       bivwak   lok   kuntri

       four   should   soup   glamour   (journey°)
       o   u   ɯ   ə   ə
       for   ʃud   sɯp   glamər   jərni
       for   shuud   soop   glamor   jurni

       out
       ɑɪ
       ɑɪt
       out

ow 4	is pronounced ⎱ ways in ⎰	knowledge ɒ nɒlij nolej	know o no noe	bellows ə beləs₂ (belos)
		now aɪ naɪ nou		

oy 2	is pronounced ⎱ ways in ⎰	coyote ɑ́ kɑ́ot kieoet	boys ɔ́ bɔ́z boiz	

pb 1	is pronounced ⎱ way in ⎰	cupboard b kʊbərd kubord		

ph 3	is pronounced ⎱ ways in ⎰	naphtha p napɸə napthha	graphic f grafik grafik	nephew v neviu₂ (nevue)

pn 1	is pronounced ⎱ way in ⎰	pneumatic n niumatik nuematik		

pp 1	is pronounced ⎱ way in ⎰	happy p hapi hapi		

ps 1	is pronounced ⎱ way in ⎰	psalm s sɑm saam		

pt 1	is pronounced⎫ way in ⎬	receipt t risɛt reseet	

| **rh** 1 | is pronounced⎫ way in   ⎬ | rhyme r rám riem | |

| **rr** 1 | is pronounced⎫ way in   ⎬ | carry r kari karri | |

| **rs** 2 | is pronounced⎫ ways in   ⎬ | worsted s wustid wuusted | hors d'oeuvre r ɔr d'ərv or d'urv |

| **rt** 1 | is pronounced⎫ way in   ⎬ | mortgage r mɔrgij morgej | |

| **sc** 4 | is pronounced⎫ ways in   ⎬ | viscount k vákaɪnt viekount | scene s sɛn seen | discern z dizərn dizurn |

crescendo
ʃ
krəʃendo
kreshendoe

| **se** 1 | is pronounced⎫ way in   ⎬ | nauseous ʃ nɔʃəs naushus | |

sh	is pronounced⎫	she
1	way in ⎭	ʃ
		ʃɛ
		shee

si	is pronounced⎫	business	pension
3	ways in ⎭	z	ʃ
		biznis	penʃən
		biznis	penshon

occasion
ʒ
əkaʒən
okaezhon

sk	is pronounced⎫	ski
1	way in ⎭	ʃ
		ʃɛ₂
		(shee)

sl	is pronounced⎫	aisle
1	way in ⎭	l
		ɑ̈l
		iel

sn	is pronounced⎫	demesne
1	way in ⎭	n
		dimɑn
		demaen

sp	is pronounced⎫	raspberry
1	way in ⎭	z
		razberi
		razberi

ss	is pronounced⎫	less	scissors	issue
3	ways in ⎭	s	z	ʃ
		les	sizərz	iʃɯ
		les	sizorz	ishoo

st is pronounced⎫ listen
1 way in   ⎭ s
                      lisən
                      lisen

sw is pronounced⎫ sword
1 way in   ⎭ s
                      sord
                      sord

tb is pronounced⎫ hautboy
1 way in   ⎭ b
                      hobɔ
                      hoeboi

te is pronounced⎫ righteous
1 way in   ⎭ c̓
                      rác̓əs
                      riechus

th	is pronounced⎫	thyme	things	that
4	ways in ⎭	t	ħ	ħ
		tám	ħiŋz	ħat
		tiem	thhingz	that

posthumous
c̓
pɒscuməs
poschuumus

ti	is pronounced⎫	nation	equation
3	ways in ⎭	ʃ	ʒ
		nɑʃən	ikwɑʒən
		naeshon	ekwaezhon

question
c̓
kwesc̓ən
kweschon

tt is pronounced⎫ little
1 way in   ⎭ t
                     litəl
                     litel

tw is pronounced⎫ two
1 way in   ⎭ t
                     tɯ
                     too

ua	is pronounced⎫	guarantee	guard	piquant
3	ways in ⎭	a	ɑ	ə
		garəntɛ	gɑrd	pɛkənt
		garrantee	gard	peekant

ue	is pronounced⎫	guess	tissue	true
5	ways in ⎭	e	u	ɯ
		ges	tiʃu	trɯ
		ges	tishuu	troo

	lacquer	(guerdon*)	due
	ə	ə	iu
	lakər	gərdən	diu
	laker	gurdon	due

uh	is pronounced⎫	buhl	buhr*
2	ways in ⎭	ɯ	ə
		bɯl	bər
		bool	bur

ui	is pronounced⎫	built	mosquito	fruit
5	ways in ⎭	i	ɛ	ɯ
		bilt	məskɛto	frɯt
		bilt	moskeetoe	froot

	guiding	suit
	á	iu
	gádiŋ	siut
	gieding	suet

| uo
2 | is pronounced
ways in | buoy
ɯ
buɪ₂
(booy) | liquor
ə
likər
likor |

| ut
1 | is pronounced
way in | debut
ɯ
dibɯ
debue | |

| uy
2 | is pronounced
ways in | plaguy
i
plɑgi
plaegi | buy
ɑ́
bɑ́
bie |

| vv
1 | is pronounced
way in | navvy
v
navi
navi | |

| wh
2 | is pronounced
ways in | whelk
w
wilk₂
(wilk) | who
h
hɯ
hoo |

| wr
1 | is pronounced
way in | write
r
rɑ́t
riet | |

| ye
1 | is pronounced
way in | dye
ɑ́
dɑ́
die | |

| zi
1 | is pronounced
way in | brazier
ʒ
braʒər
braezher | |

zj	is pronounced ⎤	muzjik₄
1	way in ⎦	ʒ
		muʊʒik
		moozhik

zs	is pronounced ⎤	britzska
1	way in ⎦	s
		britskə
		britska

zv	is pronounced ⎤	rendezvous
1	way in ⎦	v
		rɑndəvuɯ
		raandevoo

zz	is pronounced ⎤	puzzle
1	way in ⎦	z
		pʊzəl
		puzel

All other spellings

a'a
2
is pronounced ⎫
ways in ⎭

ma'am	ma'am
a	ɑ
mam	mɑm₂
mam	(maam)

a-e
7
is pronounced ⎫
ways in ⎭

have	are	ate	made
a	ɑ	e	ɑ
hav	ɑr	et₂	mad
hav	ar	(et)	maed

image	false	nuisance
i	ɔ	ə
imij	fɔls	niusəns
imej	fauls	nuesans

a-u
1
is pronounced ⎫
way in ⎭

plaguing
ɑ
plɑgiŋ
plaeging

a-ue
3
is pronounced ⎫
ways in ⎭

harangue	barque₂	plague
a	ɑ	ɑ
hərɑŋ	bɑrk	plɑg
harang	bark	plaeg

agh
2
is pronounced ⎫
ways in ⎭

shillelagh	shillelagh
i	ə
ʃilɑli₂	ʃilɑlə
(shilaeli)	shilaela

ai-e
2
is pronounced ⎫
ways in ⎭

raise	aisle
ɑ	á
rɑz	ál
raez	iel

aigh
1
is pronounced ⎫
way in ⎭

straight
ɑ
strɑt
straet

anc
1
is pronounced⎤
way in ⎦

blanc-mange
ə
blə-mɑnʒ
bla-maanzh

aou
2
is pronounced⎤
ways in ⎦

caoutchouc   caoutchouc
ɯ   aʊ
kɯċuk   kaʊċɯk₂
koochuuk   (kouchook)

au-e
5
is pronounced⎤
ways in ⎦

gauge   because   because
ɑ   ɒ   ɔ
gɑj   biknz₂   bikɔz
gaej   (bekoz)   bekauz

because   mauve
ʊ   o
bikʊz₃   mov
(bekuz)   moev

augh
1
is pronounced⎤
way in ⎦

taught
ɔ
tɔt
taut

awe
1
is pronounced⎤
way in ⎦

awe
ɔ
ɔ
au

aye
2
is pronounced⎤
ways in ⎦

aye₂   aye
ɑ   ȧ
ɑ   ȧ
ae   ie

ayo
1
is pronounced⎤
way in ⎦

mayor
ɑ
mɑr₂
(maer)

cch
l is pronounced ⎱ bacchanal
way in ⎰ k
bakənəl
bakanal

chm
l is pronounced ⎱ drachm
way in ⎰ m
dram
dram

chsi
l is pronounced ⎱ fuchsia
way in ⎰ ʃ
fiuʃə
fuesha

cht
l is pronounced ⎱ yacht
way in ⎰ t
yɒt
yot

chth
l is pronounced ⎱ chthonian
way in ⎰ ħ
ħoniən
thhoenian

ckg
l is pronounced ⎱ blackguard
way in ⎰ g
blagɑrd
blagard

dding
l is pronounced ⎱ studdingsail
way in ⎰ n
stʊnsəl
stunsel

é
l is pronounced ⎱ attaché
way in ⎰ ɑ
atəʃɑ
atashae

e-e	is pronounced⎫	ledge	there	college
6	ways in ⎭	e	a	i
		lej	ħar	kɒlij
		lej	thaer	kolej

	these	license	(were*)
	ɛ	ə	ə
	ħɛz	lásəns	wər
	theez	liesens	wur

ê-e	is pronounced⎫	fête₂
1	way in ⎭	ɑ
		fɑt
		faet

e'e	is pronounced⎫	e'er	e'en
2	ways in ⎭	ɑ	ɛ
		ɑr	ɛn
		aer	een

e-es	is pronounced⎫	belles lettres
1	way in ⎭	e
		bel-letr
		bel-letr

e-ue	is pronounced⎫	cheque₂
1	way in ⎭	e
		ćek
		chek

ea-e	is pronounced⎫	cleanse	leave	hearse*
3	ways in ⎭	e	ɛ	ə
		klenz	lɛv	hərs
		klenz	leev	hurs

ea-ue	is pronounced⎫	league
1	way in ⎭	ɛ
		lɛg
		leeg

eau 3	is pronounced ways in ⎫⎬⎭	bureaucracy ɒ biʉrɒkrəsi buerokrasi	beau o bo boe	beauty ɪu bɪuti bueti

ée 1	is pronounced way in ⎫⎬⎭	matinée ɑ matɑnɑ matinae

ee-e 1	is pronounced way in ⎫⎬⎭	cheese ɛ ćɛz cheez

eew 1	is pronounced way in ⎫⎬⎭	leeward ɯ lɯərd loo.erd

ehea 1	is pronounced way in ⎫⎬⎭	forehead i fɔrid fored

ei-e 2	is pronounced ways in ⎫⎬⎭	seine ɑ sɑn saen	receive ɛ risɛv reseev

eigh 2	is pronounced ways in ⎫⎬⎭	weigh ɑ wɑ wae	height á hát hiet

eu-e 1	is pronounced way in ⎫⎬⎭	deuce ɪu dɪus dues

ewe 1	is pronounced way in	ewe iu iu ue	
ey-e 1	is pronounced way in	eyre ɑ ar aer	
eye 1	is pronounced way in	eye ɑ́ ɑ́ ie	
eyo 1	is pronounced way in	eyot ɑ at$_2$ (aet)	
½gn 2	is pronounced ways in	vignette n vinyet vinyet	vignette y vinyet vinyet
hau 1	is pronounced way in	exhaust ɔ igzɔst egzaust	
hei 1	is pronounced way in	heir ɑ ɑr aer	
hou 2	is pronounced ways in	silhouette u siluet siluu.et	hour aυ aυr our

i-e   is pronounced⎫   give   marine   engine
4   ways in   ⎬ ,   i   ɛ   ə.
                   giv   mərɛn   enjən
                   giv   mareen   enjin

         time
         à
         tàm
         tiem

i-ue   is pronounced⎫   meringue   bisque   antique
4   ways in   ⎬   a   i   ɛ
                   məraŋ   bisk   antɛk
                   merang   bisk   anteek

         oblique
         à
         əblàk$_2$
         (obliek)

ia-e   is pronounced⎫   marriage
1   way in   ⎬   i
                   marij
                   marrej

ie-e   is pronounced⎫   sieve   believe
2   ways in   ⎬   i   ɛ
                   siv   bilɛv
                   siv   beleev

ieu   is pronounced⎫   lieu
1   way in   ⎬   ɯ
                   lɯ
                   loo

iew   is pronounced⎫   view
1   way in   ⎬   iɯ
                   viɯ
                   vue

igh **1**	is pronounced⎫ way in ⎭	high *a* h*a* hie		

½i-o **2**	is pronounced⎫ ways in ⎭	iron ə *a*ərn ie.ern	iron *a* *a*ərn ie.ern

½le **2**	is pronounced⎫ ways in ⎭	people l pɛpəl peepel	people ə pɛpəl peepel

lfp **1**	is pronounced⎫ way in ⎭	halfpenny ɑ hɑpeni haepeni

½m **2**	is pronounced⎫ ways in ⎭	criticism m kritəsizəm kritisizem	criticism ə kritəsizəm kritisizem

½ñ **2**	is pronounced⎫ ways in ⎭	cañon n kanyən kanyon	cañon y kanyən kanyon

o-e **6**	is pronounced⎫ ways in ⎭	gone ɒ gɒn$_2$ gon	gone ɔ gɔn (gaun)	some ʊ sʊm sum
	more o mor mor	move ɯ mɯv moov	welcome ə welkəm welcom	(worse*) ə wərs wurs

½o-e	is pronounced⎫	one	one
2	ways in ⎭	w	ʊ
		wʊn	wʊn
		wun	wun

o'e	is pronounced⎫	o'er
1	way in ⎭	o
		or
		or

o-o	is pronounced⎫	colonel*
1	way in ⎭	ə
		kərnəl
		kurnel

o-ue	is pronounced⎫	catalogue	torque	tongue
4	ways in ⎭	ɒ	ɔ	ʊ
		katəlɒg₂	tɔrk	tʊŋ
		katalog	tork	tung

		rogue
		o
		rog
		roeg

oa-e	is pronounced⎫	coarse
1	way in ⎭	o
		kors
		kors

oeu	is pronounced⎫	manoeuvre₂
1	way in ⎭	ɯ
		mənɯvər
		manoover

½oi	is pronounced⎫	memoir	memoir
3	ways in ⎭	w	ɑ
		memwɑr	memwɑr
		memwar	memwar

memoir
    ɔ
memwɔr₂
(memwor)

½oi-e 2	is pronounced ⎫ ways in ⎭	repertoire w repərtwɑr repertwar	repertoire ɑ repərtwɑr repertwar	
oi-e 2	is pronounced ⎫ ways in ⎭	porpoise ə pɔrpəs porpus	noise j̇ nj̇z noiz	
ois 1	is pronounced ⎫ way in ⎭	chamois i ʃami shami		
½ois 2	is pronounced ⎫ ways in ⎭	patois w patwɑ patwaa	patois ɑ patwɑ patwaa	
oo-e 1	is pronounced ⎫ way in ⎭	loose ɯ lɯs loos		
ooh 2	is pronounced ⎫ ways in ⎭	pooh u pu₂ (puu)	pooh ɯ pɯ poo	
ou-e 4	is pronounced ⎫ ways in ⎭	course o kors kors	route ɯ rɯt root	scourge* ə skərj skurj

house
aɪ
haɪs
hous

oue is pronounced ⎱ denouement
1 way in ⎰ ɯ
dɑnɯmɑn
daenoomaan

ough is pronounced ⎱ thought | though | through
4 ways in ⎰ ɔ | o | ɯ
ħɔt | ħo | ħrɯ
thhaut | thoe | thhroo

bough
aɪ
baɪ
bou

ougha is pronounced ⎱ brougham
1 way in ⎰ ɯ
brɯm₂
(broom)

oui is pronounced ⎱ bouillon
1 way in ⎰ u
bulyɒn
buulyon

oup is pronounced ⎱ coup
1 way in ⎰ ɯ
kɯ
koo

ous is pronounced ⎱ rendezvous
1 way in ⎰ ɯ
rɑndəvɯ
raandevoo

out
1 — is pronounced 1 way in

ragout
ɯ
ragɯ
ragoo

oux
1 — is pronounced 1 way in

billet-doux
ɯ
bili-dɯ
bili-doo

owa
1 — is pronounced 1 way in

toward
o
tord
tord

owe
1 — is pronounced 1 way in

owe
o
o
oe

oy-e
1 — is pronounced 1 way in

gargoyle
ɔ̣
gɑrgɔ̣l
gargoil

phth
2 — is pronounced 2 ways in

phthisic	phthisis
t	ħ
tiẓik	ħɑ́sis
tiẓik	thhiesis

pph
1 — is pronounced 1 way in

sapphire
f
safár
safier

psh
1 — is pronounced 1 way in

pshaw
ʃ
ʃɔ
shaɯ

're	is pronounced⎫	they're
1	way in ⎭	r
		ħɑ'r
		thae'r

½re	is pronounced⎫	centre₂	centre₂
2	ways in ⎭	r	ə
		sentər	sentər
		senter	senter

reca	is pronounced⎫	forecastle
1	way in ⎭	k
		foksəl
		foeksel

rps	is pronounced⎫	corps
1	way in ⎭	r
		kor
		kor

rrh	is pronounced⎫	myrrh
1	way in ⎭	r
		mər
		mur

sch	is pronounced⎫	schism	schwa
2	ways in ⎭	s	ʃ
		sizəm	ʃwɑ
		sizem	shwaa

sci	is pronounced⎫	conscience
1	way in ⎭	ʃ
		kɒnʃəns
		konshens

sew	is pronounced⎫	housewife
1	way in ⎭	z
		hʊzif₂
		(huzif)

ssi **2**	is pronounced ways in	mission ʃ miʃən mishon	scission ʒ siʒən sizhon	

sth **2**	is pronounced ways in	isthmus s ismʊs ismus	asthma z azmə azma	

tch **1**	is pronounced way in	match č mač mach		

thes **1**	is pronounced way in	clothes z kloz kloez		

tsw **1**	is pronounced way in	boatswain s bosən boesen		

u-e **6**	is pronounced ways in	minute i minit minit	judge ʊ jʊj juj	sure u ʃur shuur

	rule ɯ rɯl rool	pleasure ə pleʒər plezher	use iɯ iɯz uez		

u-ue **3**	is pronounced ways in	brusque ʊ brʊsk brusk	brusque u brusk₂ (bruusk)	fugue iɯ fiɯg fueg

uay 1	is pronounced⎫ way in ⎭	quay ε kε kee
ué 1	is pronounced⎫ way in ⎭	appliqué ɑ aplikɑ aplikae
uet 1	is pronounced⎫ way in ⎭	bouquet ɑ bokɑ boekae
ueu 1	is pronounced⎫ way in ⎭	liqueur* ə likər likur
ueue 1	is pronounced⎫ way in ⎭	queue ɯ kɯ kue
uey 1	is pronounced⎫ way in ⎭	plaguey₂ i plɑgi plaegi

| **ugh** 2 | is pronounced⎫ ways in   ⎭ | pugh u pu₂ (puu) | pugh ɯ pɯ poo |

| **ui-e** 3 | is pronounced⎫ ways in   ⎭ | guimpe a gamp₂ (gamp) | bruise ɯ brɯz brooz | guide ȧ gȧd gied |

uoi is pronounced⎤ quoin
1 way in   ⎦   ɔ̣
                      kɔ̣n
                      koin

uoi-e is pronounced⎤ turquoise
1 way in   ⎦   ɔ̣
                          tərkɔ̣z
                          turkoiz

uoy is pronounced⎤ buoy
1 way in   ⎦   ɔ̣
                      bɔ̣
                      boi

've is pronounced⎤ we've
1 way in   ⎦   v
                      wɛ'v
                      wee'v

½wh is pronounced⎤ which   which
2 ways in   ⎦   w   h
                        hwic̣   hwic̣
                        which   which

½x is pronounced⎤ next   exact   next
6 ways in   ⎦   k   g   s
                        nekst   igzakt   nekst
                        nekst   egzakt   nekst

exact	luxury	luxurious
z	ʃ	ʒ
igzakt	lʊkʃəri	lʊgʒuriəs
egzakt	luksheri	lugzhuurius

½xi is pronounced⎤ noxious   noxious
2 ways in   ⎦   k   ʃ
                        nɒkʃəs   nɒkʃəs
                        nokshus   nokshus

y-e **2**	is pronounced ⎫ ways in ⎭	apocalypse i əpɒkəlips apokalips	type á táp tiep
yew **1**	is pronounced ⎫ way in ⎭	yew iu ıu ue	
you **1**	is pronounced ⎫ way in ⎭	you iu ıu ue	
yu-e **1**	is pronounced ⎫ way in ⎭	yule iu ıul uel	
½z **2**	is pronounced ⎫ ways in ⎭	scherzo t skertso skertsoe	scherzo s skertso skertsoe
½zz **2**	is pronounced ⎫ ways in ⎭	pizzicato t pitsəkɑto pitsikaatoe	pizzicato s pitsəkɑto pitsikaatoe

Appendix C

Suggested criteria for a phonemic notation for English for general use

Abbreviations used

SSS   Simplified Spelling Society (Great Britain)
N.S.   New Spelling, promulgated by the SSS
SSA   Simpler Spelling Association (United States)
WES   World English Spelling, promulgated by the SSA
i.t.a.   Initial Teaching Alphabet (Sir James Pitman)
i.t.m. initial teaching medium (generic term)
T.O.   traditional orthography

Summary

    I   Sounds
   II Symbols
  III Assignment of symbols to sounds
  IV Influence of purpose

Illustrative application of criteria
   V To N.S. (SSS) and WES (SSA)

Criteria

I. Sounds
    A. A notation for general use should be phonemic rather than phonetic, i.e.:
       1. Should make all those distinctions and only those distinctions which are semantically significant.
       2. Should make only those distinctions readily recognizable by the average untrained ear.

157

B. The 40 sounds distinguished by Pitmanic shorthand, commonly classed as 24 consonants, 12 vowels, and 4 diphthongs, as exemplified below, using the SSA phonemic alphabet:

1. Are common to N.S. and WES, and to i.t.a.
2. Are the only phonemic basis for writing English which has been proved in practical experience by millions of writers for more than a century.

Sound	As in	Sound	As in
24 consonants		*12 vowels*	
p	*p*in, cu*p*	a	*a*m, p*a*t; *a*sk
b	*b*in, cu*b*	ɑ	*a*lms, p*a*rt, m*a*
t	*t*en, be*t*	e	*e*dge, l*e*t
d	*d*en, be*d*	ɐ	*a*ge, l*a*te, m*ay*; *ai*r
k	*c*ome, ba*ck*	i	*i*s, s*i*t; an*y*
g	*g*um, ba*g*	ɛ	*ea*se, s*ea*t, m*e*
f	*f*an, sa*f*e	ɒ	*o*dd, n*o*t
v	*v*an, sa*v*e	ɔ	*aw*ed, n*aught*, psh*aw*
ꜩ	*th*igh, ba*th*	ʊ	*u*p, t*o*n
ħ	*th*y, ba*the*	o	*o*pen, t*o*ne, sh*ow*
s	*s*eal, ra*c*e	u	f*u*ll, sh*ou*ld
z	*z*eal, rai*s*e	ɯ	f*oo*l, sh*oe*d, sh*oe*
ʃ	a*ss*ure, ru*sh*		
ʒ	a*z*ure, rou*ge*	*4 diphthongs*	
ć	*ch*oke, ri*ch*	á	*ai*sle, p*i*nt, b*y*
j	*j*oke, ri*dge*	aɪ	*ow*l, p*ou*nd, b*ough*
m	*m*et, hi*m*	ɉ	*oi*l, p*oi*nt, b*oy*
n	*n*et, thi*n*	ɯ	*u*sed, p*u*re, d*ue*
ŋ	i*nk*, thi*ng*		
l	*l*aid, dea*l*		
r	*r*aid, dea*r*		
w	*w*et, *w*e		
y	*y*et, *y*e		
h	*h*ead, *h*e		

C. In addition to these 40 sounds, the sound of schwa (as in *a*bout, f*u*rther, dat*a*), usually omitted in shorthand, must be provided for in longhand writing or printing: either—

1. By a specific character, which would change the T.O. forms of thousands of words unnecessarily; or
2. By retaining, in general, any single vowel letter of T.O., a solution which materially increases compatibility (III E).

D. Application of this basic code to particular words should maintain distinctions which a large number of cultivated speakers do make, even tho another large number of cultivated speakers do not make them — e.g.:
   1. Writing postvocalic /r/, which "r-keepers" pronounce but which "r-droppers" omit (as in *far*) or reduce to schwa (as in *near*).
   2. Writing *wh* (for /hw/) altho some speakers, especially southern British, do not distinguish it from /w/.
   3. Distinguishing the vowel of *father* and *calm* from the vowel of *bother* and *comma,* as in most British pronunciation, altho general American pronunciation does not make this distinction. This has the added advantage that (except before *r* and occasionally after *w*) it follows quite closely the T.O. spellings with *a* and *o* respectively.

II. Symbols

A. The symbols for a phonemic notation may be derived from one of three sources:
   1. *Standardizing* the Roman alphabet, by assigning to each single letter, and to each digraph selected to represent those sounds for which the available single letters do not suffice, a single sound, keeping strictly within the resources of the universally available Roman alphabet; as exemplified by N.S. and WES.
      a. A further simplification may be effected by restricting the forms of all characters, for teaching purposes at least, to a single form approximating lower-case print, thus avoiding for the time being the confusion involved in use of four alphabets, upper-case and lower-case, print and script, often differing significantly in details.

      b. For most general-use purposes, the burden of proof is strongly on those who would permit any symbol whatsoever, whether for a specific sound or as a diacritic, which is not now available on the standard typewriter keyboard and/or in the ordinary printer's font.

    2. *Supplementing* the Roman alphabet, by assigning to each of the 23 useful letters (exclusive of *c*, *q*, and *x*) a single invariable value, and creating some 17 or more new symbols, as exemplified by i.t.a. or Dr. Laubach's *English the New Way*, or the SSA phonemic alphabet, by

      a. Ligatures or graphic blends of existing letters, and/or

      b. Existing letters modified by diacritics, and/or

      c. New characters typographically congruous with the Roman alphabet. Discussion of the canons of design of the Roman alphabet is outside the scope of this statement.

    3. *Supplanting* the Roman alphabet, by creating and making available on typewriters and composing machines thruout the world some 41 wholly new characters, quite independent of the Roman alphabet, as specified by Shaw for his Proposed British Alphabet.

      a. This is an interesting philosophic speculation, but completely unrealistic in that it eliminates the factor of "self-reading" compatibility (III E) indispensable to the concurrent use involved in the process of introduction.

      b. A phonemic notation of *shorthand signs*, for *personal writing* quite apart from typing or printing, is of course not merely conceivable but highly valuable.

III. Assignment of symbols to sounds

  A. Symbols for sounds

    1. Should provide, in general, only one symbol for each sound.

      a. This is important primarily for *writing*.

      b. The burden of proof is on those who would employ more than one symbol.

2. Should regard so far as practicable, whether in selection of digraphs or diacritics or design of new letters, the predominant T.O. spellings of sounds. These are not always the predominant pronunciations of spellings (III C 4).

B. Sounds for symbols
   1. Should assign, so far as practicable, only one sound to each symbol.
      a. This is important primarily for *reading*.
      b. The burden of proof is on those who would permit more than one sound.
   2. Should regard, so far as practicable, the predominant T.O. pronunciations of spellings. These are not always the predominant T.O. spellings of sounds (III C 4).

C. Data regarding the relative frequency of particular phonemes and/or graphemes in T.O. are an important factor in designing any phonemic notation for general use.
   1. Relative frequency of *occurrences* of phonemes and/or graphemes in *connected matter* is, in general, more important than
   2. Relative frequency of *items*, i.e., *different words* in which they occur.
   3. Occurrences are, in general, more important for *reading*, and items for *writing*, i.e., spelling.
   4. Distinguish clearly between the commonest spellings of phonemes and the commonest pronunciations of graphemes. Thus, the predominant spellings of the name-sounds of the letters A, E, U are *a*, *e*, *u*, respectively; but the greatly predominant pronunciations of the letters *a*, *e*, *u* are as in *bat*, *bet*, *but* respectively. Similarly, the commonest spelling of the phoneme /z/ is *s*, but the commonest pronunciation of *s* is /s/.

D. Uniformity
   1. Uniformity of symbolization, despite regional variations in pronunciation, is greatly facilitated by the tendency of each region to attach its own values to the symbols, especially for the vowel sounds.
   2. For a textbook or dictionary key to pronunciation,

to be read rather than written, three ambivalent symbols may be justified to maintain uniformity in printing.

 a. For the vowel of *ask, bath, aunt,* which varies regionally but also unpredictably between the vowels of *cam* and *calm,* with the former more usual in the United States.
 b. For the vowel of *air, care, their,* which varies regionally between the vowels of *bat, bet,* or *bait;* use of the latter, as in Pitman Shorthand, causing the least confusion.
 c. For the high front unstressed vowel, which Sir James Pitman has aptly named *schwi,* which combines most of the shortness of *i* in *bit* with much of the closeness of *ee* in *beet* — heard in the last vowel of *any,* the first vowel of *believe.*

E. Compatibility with T.O.

 1. To be acceptable for general use, a phonemic notation must achieve a "self-reading" degree of compatibility with T.O. — that is, a degree of similarity to the words and graphemes of T.O. such that the notation may be immediately readable by those familiar only with T.O., and that T.O. may be readable with little further study by those who have mastered the phonemic notation.

  a. For a spelling reform notation, such compatibility is indispensable for the use concurrently with T.O., which is involved in the process of introduction.
  b. For an i.t.m., such comptability is no less indispensable to facilitate the process of transition from the i.t.m. to T.O.

 2. So far as possible, bizarre, ambiguous, or misleading wordforms should be avoided.

  a. A Roman alphabet letter should *never* be assigned to a value wholly unrelated to its usual significations — e.g., *x* for schwa, or *q* for a value unrelated to /k/ or /w/.
  b. Similarly, misuse of upper-case or small-cap letters with a significance other than the cor-

responding lower-case letters is wholly indefensible.

3. A phonemic notation should, in applying a phonemic code
   a. Prefer as a guide to phonemic word forms the pronunciations heard in careful, deliberate speech. The suggested schwa rule (I C 2) facilitates this.
   b. Prefer as a guide, where dictionaries recognize more than one pronunciation, the one that will make the phonemic form more like T.O.; e.g., *agaen, been, naetuer,* rather than *agen, bin, naecher.*

4. Wordsigns
   a. A general purpose notation may, for some purposes, substantially enhance compatibility by retaining as wordsigns or sight words the T.O. forms for a *limited* number of high frequency words. (See for example VI C 6.)

5. For a grapheme:
   a. Maximum compatibility is quite obviously a choice of the most-used symbol, whether single letter or digraph, *provided* this is sufficiently unambiguous to be suitable (III A 2, III B 2, III C 4).
   b. The second degree of compatibility is choice of the most-used letter or letters differently arranged or doubled — e.g., *ae* instead of *a* plus *consonant* plus *e* (*daet* instead of *date*), *aa, uu.*

6. For a word:
   a. Maximum compatibility is of course identity with T.O. — e.g., *and, our, see, himself, value.*
   b. The second degree of compatibility might be either the same letters in the same order, merely omitting a silent letter or letters (most often *e*) — e.g., *hav, giv, hed, hart, frend, gest, bilding, bom;* or the same letters and the same length with silent *e* transposed — e.g., *maed, heer, liek, hoem, ues* (noun).
   c. Other elements of compatibility are the same

letters in the same order except for doubling —
e.g., *hee, mee, doo, morral;* and similar read-
justments without introducing letters not already represented in the word — e.g., *faather,
shuud, throo.*

7. Measurement of compatibility
    a. For the no-new-letter, *standardizing* type of
    notation, the degree of compatibility resulting
    from the several decisions involved in the basic
    notation and subsequent modifications may be
    expressed in terms of the number of running
    words per 100,000 running words, which retain
    their exact T.O. forms, as determined from
    Dewey's *Relativ frequency of English speech
    sounds.*
    b. For the *supplementing* type of notation, meas-
    urement of compatibility inevitably involves
    a subjective factor, since about 20% of all
    phonemes will be represented by supple-
    mentary characters, of varying degrees of simi-
    larity to T.O., with the result that some 70% of
    running words contain at least one such sup-
    plementary character.

F. Simplicity
    1. A general-purpose phonemic notation should in-
    volve as few rules or exceptions, alternative spell-
    ings, or ambiguous pronunciations as possible.
    However:
        a. A wholly simple one-sound, one-symbol nota-
        tion *employing no new letters* will fall short of a
        satisfactory degree of compatibility, and
        b. Once the basic 40-sounds, 40-symbols structure
        has been determined, all further gains in com-
        patibility must come from concessions from
        strictly phonemic symbolization, with a cor-
        responding departure from complete simplicity
        (V C 5, V D 2).
    2. This equation between simplicity and compati-
    bility is the final, most searching test of the validity

of a phonemic notation, for whatever purpose (*"Erst in Einschränkung erscheint der Meister"*).

IV. Influence of purpose

  A. Under present circumstances, no one phonemic notation can conceivably be best for all purposes. The purpose for which the notation is chiefly intended will significantly affect the application of such criteria as

    1. Number of sounds to be distinguished.

    2. Choice between a *standardizing*-type (no-new-letter) notation or a *supplementing*-type (one-sound, one-symbol) notation.

    3. Admission of alternative symbolizations, dependent on the relative emphasis on reading, writing, or learning.

  B. A *spelling reform notation*, to be written as well as read by the general public, must emphasize maximum simplicity — that is, a minimum of rules or exceptions or alternatives, even at some expense of compatibility.

    1. For the immediate future, to have any significant impact on the present or immediately succeeding generation, a spelling reform notation must keep within the limitations of the Roman alphabet characters universally available on standard keyboard typewriters and in most printing plants thruout the world. The saving of letters by such a notation is, however, negligible.

    2. For a more remote period, in order to achieve the enormous possible saving of 1 letter in 6, amounting to $170 million out of every $1 billion of writing and printing costs, the supplementing type of notation (II A 2 c), with single characters not exceeding the normal unit widths of the existing Roman alphabet, must be adopted.

  C. A *phonemic notation for English as a second language*, as an auxiliary medium of communication, cannot take for granted that the reader or writer will usually have met a particular word orally before having occasion to read or write it — e.g., it should distinguish the two phonemes commonly spelled *th*.

D. A *notation primarily for an i.t.m.* should give added emphasis to compatibility, even at some expense of simplicity.
1. Such emphasis will be chiefly, by rules or exceptions, *based on T.O. practice* rather than on *phonemic cues.*
2. Such concessions from phonemic writing will be least objectionable in an i.t.m. because
   a. Ease of transition to reading and writing T.O. is of paramount importance, and such concessions serve to introduce the problems of transition.
   b. Mistakes due to wrong choice of alternatives during the temporary period of writing the i.t.m. are of no lasting importance.
3. An i.t.m. should avoid or minimize wordsigns or similar sight words which disregard or contradict general rules.
4. An i.t.m., to be used chiefly in instructional materials and in the classroom, may be justified in employing supplementary characters, to the extent that they prove advantageous.
E. If proved feasible, however, an i.t.m. of the standardizing no-new-letter type offers certain important advantages:
1. In the classroom
   a. No learning and practicing of non-Roman characters, to be later discarded. (A detached ligature under any digraph, to be used briefly at its first introduction, suffices to identify it unmistakably as a single unitary symbol.)
   b. Ease of preparing supplementary instructional materials on a standard typewriter.
   c. Use of the standard keyboard typewriter as an instrument of instruction from the very beginning.
2. For one who has learned English as a second language by the aid of such an i.t.m. to the point where he can speak it and *read* T.O., the possibility to shrug off the considerable added burden of learn-

ing to *write*, i.e., to spell, T.O., and continue to write phonemically.

3. Incidentally, for the adult individual impatient with the idiosyncrasies of T.O., ease of carrying over phonemic forms into his own personal writing.

Illustrative application of criteria

V. Criteria applied to N.S. (SSS) and WES (SSA)
(Statements involving frequencies of phonemes or graphemes are based on Dewey's *Relativ frequency of English speech sounds*, or *Relative frequency of English spellings*.)

A. Sounds. Phonemically, the basic codes of N.S. and WES are in complete agreement with each other (and with i.t.a.).

B. Symbols. Both N.S. and WES keep strictly within the limitations of the Roman alphabet, permitting use of Roman alphabet capitals if desired.

C. Assignment of symbols to sounds

1. N.S. and WES (and i.t.a.) are in complete agreement as to the sounds to which they assign 23 of the 26 Roman alphabet letters:

Letter	As in	Letter	As in
a	b*a*t	n	*n*et
b	*b*in	o	n*o*t
d	*d*en	p	*p*in
e	b*e*t	r	*r*aid
f	*f*an	s	*s*eal
g	*g*um	t	*t*en
h	*h*ead	u	b*u*t
i	b*i*t	v	*v*an
j	*j*oke	w	*w*et
k	*c*ome	y	*y*et
l	*l*aid	z	*z*eal
m	*m*et		

2. N.S. and WES agree as to 13 of the 17 symbols for the remaining 17 sounds of the basic 40:

	Symbol	As in	Symbol	As in
	ch	*ch*oke	ae	*age*
(N.S.)	dh	*th*y	ee	*ea*se
(WES)	th	"	ie	*ai*sle
	ng	thi*ng*	oe	*o*pen
	sh	a*ss*ure	ue	*u*sed
(N.S.)	th	*th*igh	aa	*a*lms
(WES)	thh	"	au	a*w*ed
	zh	a*z*ure	oi	*oi*l

	Symbol	As in
(N.S.)	oo	f*u*ll
(WES)	uu	"
	ou	o*w*l
(N.S.)	uu	f*oo*l
(WES)	oo	"

3. Treatment of the unstressed vowels, more particularly schwa, altho stated a little differently in N.S. and WES, is substantially the same.

4. The basic code, plus the general schwa rule, as above:
   a. As employed by N.S., retains the exact T.O. forms of about 20,500 words, or 1 word in 5.
   b. As employed by WES, retains the exact T.O. forms of about 23,650 words (excluding the word *the*, dealt with under V C 6 b, below), a result due chiefly to substitution of *th* for *dh* for the voiced phoneme.

5. Concessions from strictly phonemic writing (substantially the same in N.S. and WES):

wh	for hw
nk	for ngk
ar	for aar
or	for aur

or   for oer
ur   for stressed schwa before /r/
er   for unstressed schwa before /r/
e   for unstressed /i/ in prefix syllables be-,
            de-, pre-, re-, e-, ex-
e   for unstressed /i/ in suffix syllables -es(/ez/),
            -ed, -est, -less, -ness

These 9 concessions retain the exact T.O. forms of about 4,600 additional words.

6. Wordsigns
   a. N.S. employs 11 wordsigns: 8 (*to, a, I, be, he, we, me, she*) as in T.O., totaling about 8,700 words; 3 others (*dhe, U, wer*) totaling about 8,400 words.
   b. WES rejects the wordsign principle, but by applying the general rule for unstressed schwa, writes 3 words (*the, to, a*) totaling about 12,350 occurrences, as in T.O.

7. Compatibility, in summary

	Words per 100,000 as in T.O.	
	N.S.	WES
V C 1–4 (basic notation)	20,500	23,650
V C 5 (concessions)	4,600	4,600
V C 6 (wordsigns, or equivalent)	8,700	12,350
	33,800	40,600

D. Influence of purpose
   1. N.S. offers only one version, presumptively suitable for spelling reform, World English, and/or an i.t.m. — a simple position, which has much to commend it.
   2. WES as an i.t.m. accepts, on the basis of the judgment and experience of Sir James Pitman's i.t.a., and for the sake of the closest possible agreement with i.t.a. for experimental comparisons, 3 major and 4 minor modifications, all based on *T.O. prac-*

tice rather than on *phonemic cues.* Together these substantially increase compatibility with T.O., thus further facilitating the all-important transition to T.O.

		As in T.O.
a.	Doubled consonants where T.O. has doubled consonants, including *ck*	2,000
b.	*c* for *k*, where T.O. has *c* for *k*	1,200
c.	*y* where T.O. has *y* for unstressed /i/ (or /ee/) at the end of a word or root	800
	(Less duplicate counting of above 3 effects; e.g., in *happy, cannot, county, practically*)	(400)
d.	*th* for the unvoiced phoneme as well as the voiced, except where a homograph would result	400
e.	*yoo* for *ue*, where T.O. has a *y*	–
f.	*l* syllabic (with no vowel) where T.O. has *-le* following a consonant	–
g.	*aur* for *or*, where T.O. has *a* or *au* before *r*	–
		4,000
	Compatibility of normal spelling reform version	40,600
	Net compatibility of WES i.t.m. version	44,600

In addition, these 7 modifications improve the compatibility, without however resulting in exact T.O. forms, of about 16,900 additional words per 100,000; a total improvement of some 61,500 wordforms per 100,000.

The case against spelling reform

The principal arguments against spelling reform, with their corollaries, are summarized below, with appropriate comments and quotations:

1. *Statement:* Phonetic spelling would obscure the derivation of words.

   Corollary: To memorialize historic facts of a language is a legitimate or primary function of a current orthography.

Comments

The primary purpose of spelling is to record speech, which *is* the language.

> The true and sole office of alfabetic writing is faithfully and intelligibly to represent spoken speech. . . . (American Philological Association, 1876 report [see Table 4].)

The etymologist is the first to repudiate this argument.

> In the interests of etymology we ought to spell as we pronounce. To spell words as they used to be pronounced is not etymological, but antiquarian (W. W. Skeat).[2]

---

[1] Most of the references in Appendix D would employ the word "phonemic" rather than "phonetic" if written today. To avoid confusion, while quoting accurately, I have myself written "phonetic," which should likewise be understood as "phonemic."

[2] Simplified Spelling Society, *Braeking the spel* (London: Sir Isaac Pitman & Sons, Ltd., 1942), 2d cover.

Phonetic spelling would give a continuous moving picture of the whole history of each word, whereas fixed conventional spelling gives, at best, only a single still picture of one episode.

> The real etymologist, the historic student of language, is wholly independent of any such paltry assistance, and would rejoice above measure to barter every "historical" item in our spelling during the last 300 years for a strict phonetic picture of the language as spoken at that distance in the past (William Dwight Whitney).[3]

Even such etymologic information as is suggested is often in error, the result of some superficial wrong assumption, e.g.:

comptroller	island
debt	sovereign
delight	sprightly
haughty	

Such accurate information as present conventional spelling gives is now securely preserved in innumerable books, regardless of present or future spelling. The scholar does not need, the average layman does not appreciate or understand such information.

2. *Statement:* Phonetic spelling would cause serious confusion between words of like sound (homophones), now distinguished by different spellings; e.g.:

right, rite, write, wright	buy, by
cent, scent, sent	hear, here
road, rode, rowed	hour, our
sew, so, sow	knew, new
to, too, two	one, won

Corollaries: A spelling is a word. Such distinctions are an intentional or desirable feature of English spelling.

Comments

Context makes clear such distinctions in speech, in which spelling gives no help; still more so in the more deliberate

[3] Vaile, *Our accursed spelling*, p. 41.

processes of reading, with opportunity to glance backward or forward if necessary.

As against a few hundred homophones now distinguished more or less fortuitously by different spellings, there are in traditional orthography many thousands of words of like sound *and* spelling (homographs), and there is no demand to create artificial distinctions for these. A few suggestive examples are:

> *bay* (a color, a tree, a part of a building, a body of water, a prolonged bark)
> *fair* (good weather, impartial, an exposition)
> *right* (a privilege, opposite of left, opposite of wrong)
> *sound* (a condition, a noise, a body of water)
> *spring* (a season, a leap, an elastic device)
> *state* (to express in words, a condition, a unit of government)
> *can* (to be able, a container)
> *down* (a direction, soft feathers)
> *note* (a musical tone, a monetary obligation)
> *pool* (a small body of water, a game)
> *present* (a time, a gift)
> *well* (being in health, a hole in the earth)

Fries [4] reports that for the 500 most used words of English the *Oxford Dictionary* records 14,070 separate and different meanings — an average of 28 different meanings for each word.

There is another group of homographs, spelled alike but pronounced differently, occasionally confused in reading, which phonemic spelling would clearly distinguish, e.g.:

> *bow* (boe, bou); similarly *mow, row, sow*
> *close* (cloes, cloez); similarly *excuse, house, use,* etc.
> *aged* (aejd, aejed); similarly *blessed* (blest, blessed), *beloved, learned*
> *lead* (leed, led); similarly *read*
> *live* (liv, liev); *tear* (taer, teer); *wind* (wind, wiend); *wound* (wuund, wound)

[4] Charles C. Fries, *Linguistics and reading* (New York: Holt, Rinehart & Winston, 1962), p. 57.

3. *Statement:* Phonetic spelling would require all existing books to be reprinted.

Comments

Most current reading matter is ephemeral.

Books of enduring worth are constantly being reprinted in current spelling.

No one but the linguistic scholar today reads Chaucer, Spenser, Shakespeare, or even Milton in the original spelling.

Compatibility makes a *reading* knowledge of traditional orthography relatively easy.

4. *Statement:* Phonetic spelling would require a fixed standard of pronunciation that does not exist.

Comments

Accurately *phonetic* writing is neither necessary nor desirable. At the phonemic level, there does exist an acceptable standard, increasingly established by national and international radio and television. As early as 1935, the British Broadcasting Corporation had successfully established a standard, *Broadcast English,* for announcers.

So far as regional differences are concerned, the individual tends to project on to the phonemic symbol his own interpretation.

The few broad differences in pronunciation, between British and American usage, e.g.:

> either (iether, eether), clerk (clark, clurk), leisure (lezher, leezher)

will be no more confusing in phonetic spelling than in speech, or than differences in choice of words, such as *lift* for *elevator.*

Phonetic spelling would be a strong conservative factor in preventing deterioration or corruption of language. Present lack of any clearly discernible relation between the written and the spoken word conduces strongly to variation.

5. *Statement:* No one has authority to tamper with the language. "The language of Shakespeare and Milton is good enough for me."

Corollaries: The written word is the language. The language (or spelling) used by past masters of English has remained substantially static, *or* language (or spelling) evolution is a natural process, independent of human control.

Comments

Our language is speech, not spelling; the spelling is, or should be, no more than a picture (too often now it is a cartoon) of the spoken word. Change, both in language and until recently in spelling, has been continuous, both before and after Shakespeare and Milton.

Phonetic spelling would conform to and record actual change and, incidentally, would tend to reduce change by giving guidance as to pronunciation, now wholly lacking.

All evolution in spelling, thus far, has resulted from conscious, deliberate, individual choice or action.

6. *Statement:* Phonetic spelling is ugly, uncouth, grotesque.

Comments

No one would seriously claim that the particular configurations of traditional orthography, the succession of ascending, descending, and middle letters, possess any intrinsic esthetic value. The true charge against phonetic spelling is strangeness.

Many proposed phonetic alphabets have been esthetically unpleasing, due to diacritics, wrong fonts, inverted letters, non-Roman characters, etc., but there is no inherent reason why a phonetic alphabet cannot be made as esthetically pleasing as the present Roman alphabet, if it observes the same canons of design; e.g., the Simpler Spelling Association phonemic alphabet.

The i.t.m. technique, which accustoms the eye to rational forms, is one important element in breaking down the next generation's resistance to spelling reform.

7. *Statement:* It's too much trouble. I have learned to spell.

Comments

This, the inertia that dreads the effort of the change, is the main reason why the present adult generation should not be expected to change.

It is the generations of children to come who appeal to us to save them from the affliction which we have endured and forgotten (William Dwight Whitney).[5]

[5] March, *The spelling reform,* p. 35.

Appendix E

Transliteration guide from T.O. to WES, in a form consistent with i.t.a.[1]

To transliterate i.t.a. material into World English Spelling (WES), which may be written on any standard keyboard typewriter, is a comparatively simple matter.

Consider first the 44 characters of the familiar i.t.a. panel:

The 24 Roman alphabet letters of i.t.a. are assigned exactly the same values as in WES, except that r and z absorb the functions of i.t.a. ɼ and ʂ.

i.t.a.: b c d f g h j k l m n p r s t v w y z a e i o u
WES: b c d f g h j k l m n p r s t v w y z a e i o u

Of the 20 i.t.a. new characters, 13 are fairly obvious ligatures or blends of the corresponding WES digraphs, except for the WES trigraph *thh*, which is used (instead of *th*) only in rare cases when necessary to distinguish otherwise similar words, e.g., thhie: thie; teethh: teeth.

i.t.a.: æ ɶ ie œ ue wh ꜿ ꜩ ꝷ ʃ au ꟷ oi
WES: ae ee ie oe ue wh ch th(h) th sh au ou oi

Of the remaining 7 i.t.a. characters, ɼ and ʂ are suppressed, as noted above, and only 5 correspond to WES digraphs, which differ somewhat in appearance.

i.t.a.: ʒ ŋ ɑ ω ꞷ
WES: zh ng aa uu oo

[1] Based on *The i/t/a handbook for writing and spelling* (New York: i/t/a Publications, Inc., 1964), pages 13–21, as annotated on pages 22–26, and "World English Spelling (WES) for better reading" (Lake Placid Club, N.Y.: Simpler Spelling Association, 1970).

177

As in i.t.a., a doubled consonant should be written for a single sound where T.O. has a doubled consonant (see WES folder, p. 5).

The following notes on each character are arranged in the order of the *i/t/a handbook*. Since some words used as examples in the handbook involve more than one principle, this table should be supplemented, for maximum accuracy, by a copy of the handbook, in which inapplicable symbols or words have been canceled.

i.t.a.	*WES*	*Transliteration rules*	*WES examples*
a	a	Same, except before *r*	*a*t, m*a*n, *a*bout, daet*a*
		Write stressed *a* before *r* by *arr*	c*arr*y, comp*arr*ison
æ	ae	Equivalent, when stressed	*ae*j, m*ae*n, s*ae*
		In unstressed syllables, prefer usually *e*	aver*e*j, pri*e*vet
	aer	Write *aer* in air, care, their, etc., as in i.t.a.	*aer*, c*aer*, th*aer*
au	au	Equivalent	*au*thor, l*au*, *au*ll
		As in i.t.a. write *aur* only where T.O. has *a* (for most occurrences of *aur*, see under *or*)	w*aur*, w*aur*m
ɑ	aa	Equivalent, except before *r*	f*aa*ther, c*aa*m
(ɑr)	ar	Write *ar* for *aar* (95% of all occurrences)	*ar*my, m*ar*ket, f*ar*
ᴅ	(a)	Write *a* as representing American majority usage (this i.t.a. ambiguous character is not used in classroom writing)	*a*sk, *a*fter, p*a*st
b	b	Same	*b*ae, ru*bb*er, ca*b*
c	c	Same, where, and only where, T.O. has *c* for the /k/ sound	*c*aem, a*c*count, ba*c*k

i.t.a.	WES	Transliteration rules	WES examples
		Write *chh* to distinguish the Scottish aspirated *ch*	lo*chh*,* baa*chh*
ʤ	ch	Equivalent, but do not write *tch*	*ch*eck, *ch*urch; wo*ch*
d	d	Same, but do not write *dj* (see under *j*), nor *dzh* (see under *zh*)	*d*oun, la*dd*er, bi*d*
e	e	Same, but do not write *e* for *stressed* schwa (see under *ɼ*)	*e*j, h*e*d, *e*ny
ɛɛ	ee	Equivalent	*ee*ch, h*ee*r, s*ee*
f	f	Same	*f*ast, o*ff*is, *f*oetogra*f*
g	g	Same	*g*aem, ra*gg*ed, e*g*zact
h	h	Same	*h*ad, be*h*iend, *h*oo
i	i	Same, but do not write *i* for *stressed* schwa (see under *ɼ*)	*i*t, h*i*m; pr*i*tty
		Do not write *i* for the /y/ sound	span*y*el
ie	ie	Equivalent	*ie*s, t*ie*, m*ie*t
j	j	Same, but do not write *dj*	*j*ust, stae*j*; a*j*ust
k	k	Same, where T.O. has *k*, or *x* for *ks*, and for *q*	*k*eep, e*k*spect, *k*wi*ck*
l	l	Same	*l*aet, fe*ll*oe, dee*l*
m	m	Same	*m*iet, com*m*on, the*m*
n	n	Same	*n*iet, di*nn*er, the*n*
ŋ	ng	Equivalent, except before /k/	thi*ng*, goei*ng*, si*ng*gl
	nk	Before the /k/ sound, write *n* for *ng*	thi*n*k, a*n*kl, u*n*cl
o	o	Same, except before *r*	*o*n, n*o*t, w*o*z, wh*o*t
		Write stressed *o* before *r* by *orr*	bo*rr*oe, autho*rr*ity
	or	Write *or* for *aur*, except where T.O. has *a* (see under *au*)	*or*der, n*or*th, f*or*
		Write *or* also for *oer* (see WES folder, under *or*)	st*or*y, m*or*, d*or*

i.t.a.	WES	*Transliteration rules*	WES *examples*
œ	oe	Equivalent, except before *r*	*oe*ld, n*oe*t, g*oe*z
		Write *oer* by *or* (see under *or*, next above)	
ɷu	ou	Equivalent	*ou*t, n*ou*, b*ou*
ɷi	oi	Equivalent	*oi*l, p*oi*nt, b*oi*
ω	uu	Equivalent	g*uu*d, sh*uu*d, p*uu*t
ꞷ	oo	Equivalent	f*oo*d, r*oo*l, gr*oo*
		Distinguish between *oo* and *ue* as in WES folder, substantially as in *i/t/a handbook*	
p	p	Same	*p*ae, ha*pp*y, ca*p*
r	r	Same, except as under *ʌ*, next below	*r*aet, ma*rr*id, dee*r*
ʌ	(r)	Substitute *r*, as next below	
	ur	Write *stressed* schwa before *r*, always by *ur*	f*ur*ther, h*ur*, f*ur*st
	er	Write unstressed schwa before *r*, usually by *er*, unless T.O. has *a*, *i*, or *o*	furth*er*, maek*er*, mur-m*er*; calend*a*r, as-pir*i*n, parl*o*r
s	s	Same	*s*eel, le*ss*on, *s*ity, rae*s*
ʃh	sh	Equivalent	*sh*all, pre*sh*er, nae*sh*on
ʒ	zh	Equivalent, but do not write *dzh*	ple*zh*er, vi*zh*on; ju*j*
ꭍ	(z)	Substitute *z* in all cases	dae*z*, i*z*, rae*z*, sie*z*
t	t	Same, but do not write *tch*	*t*oun, le*tt*er; ma*ch*
ꚩh	th(h)	Equivalent, but write *th* except where distinction is required	*th*roo; ee*thh*er (eether)
	th	Equivalent	*th*at, ra*th*er, wi*th*
u	u	Same	*u*p, *u*ther, t*u*ch

i.t.a.	WES	Transliteration rules	WES examples
ue	ue	Equivalent	*ue*z, m*ue*zic, d*ue*, f*ue*
		As in i.t.a. write *yoo* where T.O. has *y*	*yoo*, *yoo*th
		Distinguish between *oo* and *uu* as in WES folder, substantially as in *i/t/a handbook*	
v	v	Same	*v*ast, ne*v*er, sae*v*
w	w	Same	*w*et, *w*un, k*w*iet
wh	wh	Equivalent	*wh*ich, every*wh*aer
y	y	Same initially, in words or syllables	*y*et, be*y*ond, mill*y*on
		Write *y* for /i/, where T.O. has *y*, at the end of a word or root, but not medially	pit*y*, pit*y*d, ever*y*-thing; p*i*ramid
z	z	Same, including all occurrences of *s* (see also under *s*)	*z*eel, pu*zz*l, rae*z*e*z*

For a fuller treatment of unstressed vowels, see WES folder, p. 6.

As in i.t.a., use only lower-case letter forms for the first teaching of reading and writing (see WES folder, p. 4).